for my
GRANDCHILDREN
Principles for a Successful Life

ROBERT KING

TABLE OF CONTENTS

ACKNOWLEDGEMENTS

There are so many people I would like to thank. I would like to thank them for their encouragement and understanding. I'm sure I came close to driving my wife crazy talking about "The Book." Thanks to my children and grandchildren for being my testing ground and the reason for my writing this book. Anne Stanwick was not only encouraging but typed the first few editions of the book. And a special thank you to all those who contributed to the book. With few exceptions the contributers are working and not retired. This was a consideration in asking them to contribute.

I am very grateful to Mollie Sorenson for her excellent help in formatting, proofing and very helpful suggestions. And thank you to Peggy Forney and Laurel McHargue for their assistance as well. There are many others that I would like to thank that I'm sure I've overlooked but did not mean to. So, thanks to anyone who helped me create this book.

PREFACE

To my grandchildren: it's 6 a.m. and 17 degrees (that's cold!), I am sitting out in the snow elk hunting with your dad. Actually, I am hunting at the same time as your dad. He is about 600 vertical feet above me right now. It is something we look forward to every year, but he misses you nevertheless. We're sitting waiting for other impatient hunters to chase some elk and deer toward us. It's very quiet. The birds are beginning to sing. Woodpeckers are sounding like carpenters framing a house. The squirrels are moving about tree to tree but I see no elk and no deer. I like it anyway. I have lots of time and few distractions to take time to meditate and think. The sunrise is slow to come but very beautiful. The shades of grey are replaced by blue. The sun is turning the high clouds to an orange and then gold color. The day is coming alive and as an African spiritual sings, "Day done broke into my soul …"

I'm thinking of my wonderful life and my wife Karen, your grandma you call Nini. Our wonderful life together includes you, our grandchildren, as a big part of it. We hope that you have an even better life than we have. I'm not sure what we can do to cause that to happen, although I do have a few ideas. But first, we want you to know that life is a continual learning process and we continue to learn from many sources, including you.

I don't know if or when the concepts presented here will be meaningful to you but it is better I try than not try. When I leave this earth I could leave you many things. I could leave you things such as possessions or money. But the best thing I could leave you is an understanding of the principles of life contained herein, for they will help you as long as you are on this earth. So my wish for you is that you will achieve a life that is even better than what you wish for yourself.

I'm writing this to you, my grandchildren, in the hope that it might make your life's journey a bit easier and more successful by whatever criteria you choose to use to measure success. Life isn't fair. We do not come into this world with equal physical, mental, emotional, financial or environmental circumstances. That is just the way it is. The sooner you realize and accept that fact the less difficult your life will be. What I have written for you will facilitate forward movement in your life's journey.

There is another reason I am writing this for you. I want you to know about your ancestors and where it all started for me. My dad was not born here in the United States. My dad, Al King, was born on September 15, 1907. He told me he was born in Buffalo, New York. I had no reason to doubt that this was so. He was always reluctant to answer my questions about his family. I responded to this by keeping my inquiries, which were never fully satisfied, to a minimum. Usually my questions regarding his youth were a result of my friends asking me what kind of accent he had. I never detected an accent. I told them it was a Buffalo, New York accent as he had always told me.

FOR MY GRANDCHILDREN

When I was 24 years old my mother surprised me by informing me that Dad was actually born in the village of Ladanja Dolnje, which is now in Croatia. No wonder my friends thought he had an accent!

Learning of Dad's background was a surprise. It unleashed my curiosity and with some probing, Dad did tell me some interesting stories. He remembered his village and his home that had no running water or electricity. Water was obtained from a central village well. He remembered having a garden and chickens in his small backyard.

Dad's father came to the U.S. around 1909 or 1910. My dad, at age 13, obtained a ticket to come to the U.S. (by himself) in 1920. In 1925 he joined the U.S. Army. He became a naturalized citizen of the U.S. on February 25, 1943, and changed his name from Andro Kralj to Albert King.

After being honorably discharged from the army, he looked in the newspaper want ads and noticed that barbers were in demand. So off to barber school he went. He remained a barber his entire working life and seemed to love every minute of it.

My mother was born on June 17, 1917 in Waterbury, Connecticut, maybe. One birth certificate has her name as Tessie Ponomarenko which was her mother's name as well, and probably the result of her parents not understanding how to fill out the official documents. Her father was Mike Ponomarenko. Mom said both her parents were from Russia. When she was four years old her mother died. Her father was unable to take care of his young family for financial reasons. In an effort to give his children a better life they were admitted to St. Joseph's Home (an orphanage run by the Franciscan Sisters of the Catholic Church). Mom was admitted as Ellen Pomart, when she was six years old, on October 29, 1923. She left the Home on March 29, 1934 when she was 17.

I was born on December 19th, 1943. We lived in an apartment in a private residence. Dad worked as a barber and Mom did secretarial work. I loved my parents. Out of necessity they both worked and as a result I had a lot of unsupervised time after school. At this time we lived in an apartment so small we could sit at the dining table and open the refrigerator, take pots off the stove and put dishes in the sink without getting up. When my parents were at work, I was supposed to watch over my brother which didn't always work out the way my parents expected. We watched more TV than anyone should. I almost never did my homework and I was the "King of Procrastination." I remember many times going to school not having done my homework. As a result I had sweaty pits due to the anxiety I felt anticipating a teacher asking me a question related to the homework. It seemed that in grade school I spent more time in the principal's office than his secretary.

During these years I felt like a "loser" because it seemed just about everything I did turned out poorly. So I can accurately say that for the first 20 years of my life I did the opposite of what is presented in this workbook. The point of this is to give you an understanding that I have lived on both sides of the success curve. I was a miserable failure at just about anything I did. After high school graduation I attended a community college for one semester. The reason it was only one semester was because I was on academic probation and realized that by the end of the second semester the situation would probably not have changed. It was time to leave school and earn a living. I worked low paying jobs, lived in my own apartment that didn't always have heat or hot water and couldn't afford to repair my car. I got a job with I.B.M. at the corporate headquarters in New York City delivering mail to the employees of I.B.M. It was a very interesting job. Working in the city I got to meet the top executives of I.B.M. I also drove some of the executives from New York City to Yorktown 33 miles to the north. I had an opportunity to see some photographs of these executives socializing as all deliveries went by way of the mail room. Occasionally, I got to drive Tom Watson, Jr's (the chairman of the board) and A. L. Williams' (president of I.B.M.) cars in for maintenance. It is a big mistake to let an 18-year-old behind the wheel of an expensive car. Watson drove a Lincoln Continental, the most expensive car I had ever been in. I remember thinking that it was bigger than my apartment. It started me thinking about my own situation. I was tired of worrying that I might not be able to pay the rent, have enough money to buy groceries or to pay for enough heat to be comfortable. I was tired of failing and decided to make some changes. These changes included learning about principles of human behavior, commerce and nature and use them to my benefit. Applying these changed my life for the better. When Nini and I were married we saved our money and had enough money to purchase just about anything we wanted. We lived in very nice homes. So, I have been on both sides of the bell shaped curve of success and I can tell you being on the right side of the curve is a lot better than being on the left side. The life changing principles that made this possible are contained in this workbook. I hope they will inspire you to live a successful life.

INTRODUCTION

It has been said there are three ways you can learn. The first way you can learn is from your own research and that includes reading, thinking, planning and implementing what you've learned. Hopefully this book will give you some skills and suggestions that will help you to do this throughout your life's journey. As important as school is, you probably will not learn the concepts presented in this book in the classroom. School is very important. You need to have a warehouse of information but there are other extracurricular concepts that will make your life's journey more interesting, rewarding and successful. They are contained in this book. Hopefully, this will be a starting point for you and something you will find helpful from time to time throughout your life.

The second way you can learn is through the experience of others. This is much easier and generally involves a lot less time and energy and the results can be very beneficial. You might be interested to know how to build or buy something or perhaps a field of study or a business to pursue. It is always beneficial to find others who have done what you're thinking about doing and learn from them. After all, they have already done it. Usually it costs you nothing and you can meet some very interesting people who have already done the research and will have experience from which you can learn. Never underestimate the value of your parents or relatives. They love you and have a wealth of experience and wisdom to share with you. You just have to ask them and have an open mind.

For example, you may desire to enter into a career in nursing. Your family has a friend who happens to be a nurse. It would be very helpful to speak to this person and find out information that might be helpful for you in deciding whether or not nursing is the career for you. You could ask why did they go into nursing? What do they like about nursing? What don't they like about nursing? If they had to do it over again, what would they change? These are things that will be helpful to you. Doing so would be a lot easier than the third method of learning.

The third method of learning is through your own experience. A man named Will Rogers, an American humorist, once said, "Good judgment comes from experience and a lot of that comes from bad judgment." Another way of saying that is, as my dad would describe it, "the school of hard knocks." Will Rogers described the third way as, "when you have exhausted the first two ways to learn, the third way is to pee on the electric fence." When I was growing up this was my preferred method of learning. From experience I must say that the first two methods of learning are much more efficient and less costly in so many ways.

The materials and concepts in this book are not presented in sequential order. All the concepts are important to learning the "secrets of successful living." When you understand the concepts presented you will see the sum result of implementing them is greater than any one of the concepts taken alone. This is the gestalt of the components. These concepts function as a network, there is overlapping between the concepts. This creates a synergy between the concepts and functions to make these concepts have a stronger effect. Implementing them may not result in an "Ah ha" epiphany but it will facilitate whatever it is that you are doing. Whenever you learn to play a new game you need to know two things. First, what is the objective of the game? The second is what are the rules? The content of this book is like learning a new game. The game of living a successful life. I don't mean to take this lightly because it is serious business. But there are "rules" that make the process easier.

It seems to me that life's journey consists of four phases. The first phase is *socialization*, followed by *education*, *production* and then *reflection*. Each of these phases involves the four aspects of your being: Personal, Professional, Financial and Spiritual. Understanding that these aspects exist and nurturing them is very important. Not to do so results in a life whose motto could be, "Life happens."

It is human nature to want more. Better friends, a spouse with whom to share your life's journey, a home, and a job you thoroughly enjoy, etc. I have never met anyone who said they wish they had less. I have never heard anyone say they wish they drove a car that wasn't as nice as the one they are currently driving. Or, that they would like to live in less comfortable circumstances. This isn't to imply that you should always feel that you cannot enjoy what you have and that you would only be happy if you had more. You may have a substantial amount of knowledge in a particular area but you may desire to have even greater knowledge in that area. It's all about continual improvement in all aspects of your life. It makes life more interesting and more fun. This is what a successful life includes.

So how do you achieve a successful life? It is deciding to lead a life of intention, a life that you direct. Is there a formula for success? Many are looking for such a formula and believe it must be a complicated formula that's easy to apply and guarantees success.

If something like that exists, I'm unaware of it. The truth is, there are many "formulas" for success. What follows is one of them. It is simple, easy to understand and logical, but it is not easy to apply and does not guarantee success. It requires understanding and application of the principles of human behavior, commerce and nature in a thoughtful manner.

These concepts might not be taught in school. But they relate to all that you do and make life much easier if you understand and implement them. They are principles of human behavior independent of you and me. I struggled with my life's pathway until I was in my late 20s. When I learned and applied what I'm writing to you it made a huge difference in my life. It has helped me to have a more successful business, to accomplish more, to enjoy my family (including you) and has reduced my stress level considerably. I hope you will read what I have written and think about implementing these things in a way that is natural to you and make these things part of your being. I'm sure you will benefit from doing so.

You will notice that at the end of many of the sections there will be several lines. These lines are there for you to make notes to yourself. You may use these lines to answer the following:

What does the above section mean to me?

How can I apply the principles described in my own life?

Anything else you find meaningful.

You will also notice that after some of the sections there will be brief stories written by people of various ages. These are stories of how the previous section has applied to their lives. They are written in their own words and I have included their name, age and occupation if appropriate. I did this because the contents of this book affect everyone regardless of their age or occupation.

This is not a book meant to be read through and then discarded. It is meant to be a user manual that you might refer to from time to time throughout your life to help you lead a successful life. It can provide the mortar for all the building blocks you learn in each of the phases of life and the aspects of your life.

You might read one section every week. Use the rest of the week to think about why and how to implement the section you have read in your daily life.

Some people are successful. You may as well be one of them!

COMMENTS: I restarted my college career on a full time basis when I was 21 years old. I finally learned and applied the principles contained herein. I did very well academically even though I worked full time for the first three years of my four year education. I graduated with a Bachelor of Science degree in Physical Therapy and went to work in Burbank, California where I learned what a physical therapist actually did. Two years later I moved to a small town in Missouri where I began a private practice with a friend. Three years later we moved to Omaha where we opened an outpatient office. A few years later I bought my partner's interest in the business and expanded to nine states. I personally worked in an outpatient office in Omaha and oversaw outpatient offices and contracted hospitals in other areas. Omaha was my home base. I considered all other facilities to be satellite facilities. I sold my company to a national company and found myself doing many activities which I had done as a former business owner. Research, development, sales, production and management were some of my duties. I also edited the company newsletter and visited satellite facilities (outpatient rehabilitation centers and contracted hospitals) that were not doing as well financially as the company would like. I was always a student of principles of human behavior, commerce and nature that shape our behavior. The concepts presented in this book are a result of my education, experience and thought. These concepts may or may not be the result of original thinking, but however the concepts were derived they represent behavioral models. They work. I have chosen twenty five topics. There are many more important topics. The topics included are those I think are the most important. These are not presented in an exhaustive manner. They are meant to give you a basic understanding of each principle. There are many self-help publications available to you should you want to learn more.

∼CHAPTER 1∼

THE FOUR PHASES OF LIFE

Life can be divided into four phases: socialization, education, production and reflection, as seen in figure 1.

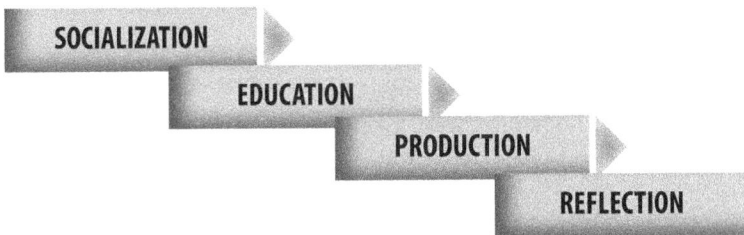

SOCIALIZATION

EDUCATION

PRODUCTION

REFLECTION

Figure 1

While these do occur in linear sequence, there is overlapping at the beginning and end of each segment as can be seen in Figure 1. A particular phase is dominant depending upon where you are in the process. Out of necessity you begin your journey in the Socialization

1

Phase. Later, you will be in the Education Phase but the process of socialization will still continue. You may have mastered getting dressed, using the toilet, and talking, but you will learn how to refine higher level socialization skills, such as communication, throughout your life. One never masters any one of these phases so well that improvement is not possible.

SOCIALIZATION

Before you started going to school you learned from your mom and dad. This is the first phase of life, the Socialization Phase. You begin by learning the basics of civilized life: appropriate use of the toilet, using a spoon and fork, saying please and thank you and how to behave. The object at this time, although you probably didn't realize it, was for everyone, you, your siblings if you had any and your parents, to get through the day in as pleasant a way as possible. This required learning the rules set by your mom and dad. The closer you followed those rules the easier it was and the more time you had for determining how you would spend your time.

Recently, we were celebrating a birthday at one of your homes. Our youngest grandchild (who shall remain nameless) is very stubborn and was slow to potty-train. Actually, he eventually potty-trained himself. While we were all enjoying sitting out on the patio, the door to the garage opened and there he was standing over a puddle. Apparently, he thought the garage floor was the best place to take care of his urgent need. While this was being cleaned up the little guy disappeared.

A few minutes later one of our older grandchildren came out to the patio and stated calmly that the little guy pooped on the living room carpet! But it gets even better. Everyone rushed to the living room to clean up the mess but not as fast as the dog!

When we got to the living room, there was no mess to be found but the dog was licking its lips! So, the Socialization Phase was not proceeding quite as rapidly as his parents would have preferred.

Socializing children is not an easy job for parents. Teaching you behaviors and values that will help you later in life is not an easy job. Not because you were so difficult, although at times you may have been, but because they were working, maintaining a household and juggling several other things at the same time. For example, your parents come home from work, prepare dinner, clean up after dinner, help you with your homework, and get everyone ready for the next day and then they send you upstairs to clean your room. When they go upstairs they may find that you didn't do a very good job cleaning your room so instead of them making you do it again they do it themselves because it's quicker. This may delay your socialization but sometimes this is the easiest way to get through the day.

EDUCATION

Hopefully you'll be prepared for the second phase of life which is Education. I'm sure you can imagine how chaotic the scene would be in kindergarten if no one at least began the Socialization Phase. The Education Phase is generally concerned about learning useful things, such as reading, math, writing, science, history and other subjects. The purpose of this is to prepare you to live independently, pay your bills and live as you wish. This doesn't happen without your active participation. Like so many things in life, only you can determine how you will benefit from any situation or experience. This phase of life is critical for those who desire to succeed. Whatever path of life you choose to follow you will need to pay the bills. The more money you make the easier it will be to pay the bills and the more choices you will have. One of the reasons determining your level of income will be how difficult it is to replace you. The more education and training you have the more difficult it will be to replace you and the greater your income will be. You should enjoy life but you should also realize that the Educational Phase of your life is very serious and should be treated so.

PRODUCTION

The third phase of life is the Production Phase. You are putting to use what you have learned in the previous phases which are socialization and education. This may be the most difficult phase because it lasts the longest and requires continual self-improvement through more education and training if you want to do well. There's a reason why graduation from high school, college or trade school is called commencement. It's because it is just the beginning. How well you do in the Production Phase of life is dependent upon what you have learned and applied in the first two phases of life. And throughout this phase of life there will be many changes, many of which you will have little or no control over that will require you to adapt by learning new skills and acquiring new or additional information.

REFLECTION

The fourth phase of life is the Reflection Phase. If you planned well enough you will actually have time to reflect on your life and life in general. Typically, your most productive years in terms of earning capacity are behind you. You may still be working but if this is the case, hopefully it is because you want to work and not because you have to work. Of course, this too, is the result of choices you made during the first three phases of your life.

It is said that for every phase of life there is a season. The more clearly you understand these concepts, the more clearly you understand the rules of the game of life. The more you understand the rules of the game, the more organized and goal oriented your life can become. The greater your chances will be for a successful life.

How can being aware of the Four Phases of Life help you?

_____

_____

_____

_____

_____

_____

_____

BRENNAN, age 8:

We had friends over and were watching a movie. My brother came in and tried to get us to play a game with him. I did not want to play the game so instead of telling him nicely I punched him.

Is it time to revisit the Socialization Phase?

STEVE GUILIANI, 8th Grade Teacher:

I like to work within the framework of rules to get things done. Knowing the phases of life helps me to be a good member of society and to be successful in achieving my goals. As an educator I am the bridge between the educational phase of life and the production phase. Today education is about problem solving. When I go into my garage I expect to find what I need within three minutes and get to work on the project at hand. I also need to do this as an educator and role model. If I cannot illustrate a point regarding problem solving within three minutes, my students will lose interest.

I am also in the production phase of life as an educator. I enjoy what I am doing and will continue to teach as long as I am able to do so. But I also realize I need to plan for the next phase of life, reflection. I have lived frugally and invest wisely so I will be able to enjoy that phase and not look back with regret.

MIKE CASCIERE, Physical Therapist:

I went to college because I knew someone who was receiving physical therapy and I learned that I could be a physical therapist with a four year degree. That was what I wanted to do.

After graduating I looked for and secured a job. That is when I realized my education was just beginning. I was amazed at how much I didn't know. There were some patients whose diagnosis or condition I didn't feel qualified to treat. I identified those areas and attended continuing education courses to address my weaknesses. Things change so rapidly that continuing is just that … continuing.

I also recognized a need for a valuable service I could provide. EMG/nerve conduction velocity. Back to continuing education to learn how to do these procedures.

I enjoy helping physicians to accurately diagnose patients. It is a higher level of skill that I can provide. Continuing education is a very important part of my career. I attend at least one annual conference and other educational opportunities to make sure I am providing services at state of the art in my areas of expertise.

COMMENTS: Had I been aware of the Four Phases of Life I might have paid a lot more attention to the second phase of life, education.

I didn't appreciate the fact that the purpose of school was to prepare me to be able to take care of myself and someday my family and be a productive member of society. For me, the Educational Phase meant I knew where I was to go every day. It was as though I was going to the baby sitter's, only better. I got to play at the playground and do arts and crafts while I attended K through 6. In 7th and 8th grades I was able to participate in more fun games and sports. In grades 9 through 12 I was able to participate in junior varsity and varsity sports. As an added bonus, the girls liked anyone who had a letter sweater! Text books that were to be used during the school year were issued the first day of school. These books were returned at the end of the school year. The typical comment when I handed my books in was, "these books look as though they've never been used." How right they were!

All this may sound like fun and it was but the day of reckoning came as I was walking down the auditorium isle to receive my diploma. I had no plans. I was accepted to a community college, the only place that would give me a chance with the grades I had.

Now, I am happy with how my life turned out, but it would have been a lot easier if I had realized the Educational Phase of my life was my job. This phase would determine what options were open for me in the next phase of life, the Phase of Production. Instead, after floundering around for four years, I had to reenter the Educational Phase of my life and prepare to make a living and be a productive member of society.

~Chapter 2~

The Four Components of You

A Greek Proverb states, "Know thyself," good advice but not easy to follow. One of the ways it becomes easier to know thyself is by understanding how human beings function. One of the things that makes us human beings is the ability to be introspective, to look into ourselves and determine why we behave as we do, what we want to get out of life and decide how to become a better person. This includes the ability to create algorithms that make it easier to understand and respond to events. An algorithm that makes sense to me is that our being can be thought of as consisting of four components, Personal, Professional, Financial and Spiritual as seen in Figure 2. This algorithm is a behavioral model. It describes behaviors which are generally observable by another person. It is for ease of discussion that these four areas are treated as though they are separate. In reality, these four areas are one and the same. Just as your nose and ear are separate, they are both a part of you. So the four areas of your being are really what constitute the whole of you.

Figure 2

PERSONAL

The Personal Component of your being contains those areas which are not included in the other areas of your being. Things such as your personality, sense of humor, the music you listen to, your friends and what you like to do for recreation are examples of what are included in the personal aspect of your being. It includes the characteristic way you behave. Are you optimistic or pessimistic? Would you be described by others as an energy giver or energy taker, a problem solver or a problem maker? How do you like to dress, what is your general approach to life? Are you emotional or cognitive? Do you see life as one of scarcity where there is a limited number of opportunities or one of abundance in the opportunities available?

Write a brief description of those things that comprise the Personal Component of your being.

_____

_____

_____

_____

_____

_____

PROFESSIONAL

The Professional Component of your being contains those things that relate to your ability to earn a living. It includes your education, both formal and informal, from preschool through college, trade school and on-the-job training. If you haven't figured it out already, your education never stops until you choose to have it stop. There are always new ways to do things, new concepts to think about, new opportunities available to you, unless you choose not to see them or take advantage of them. Some individuals choose to repeat the same year, over and over again, never learning new techniques, concepts or ideas. Some believe the additional work required to take advantage of these opportunities is worth the personal and professional growth they afford. Which will you choose?

We make a living by what we get.
We make a life by what we give.
Some succeed because they are destined to.
Most succeed because they are determined to.

Write a brief description of the Professional Component of your being *(you always have a Professional Component of your being even if you are in grade school. It is school that is your job, your Professional Component).*

_____

_____

_____

_____

_____

_____

_____

FINANCIAL

Just about everything you do costs money. Money does not make you a better person but it does give you more choices. The more money you have the more choices you'll have, therefore, the Financial Component of your being is very important. Long before you begin your professional career you will have financial choices to make. How do you use the money you acquire whether it is from gifts, allowance or work? School loans will be a big part of those financial decisions. What will be the return on your investment? In other words, what do you get for your efforts and the financial obligation for which you will be responsible?

It might seem ridiculous to think about your retirement even before you know what it is you want to do to earn a living. But being able to retire will depend upon the decisions you make now. It's likely you will need several million dollars to retire successfully. This sounds like a lot of money and it is. But it is doable if you start early and are consistent in saving. Always pay yourself first, not a car company, not an entertainment company but yourself. Paying yourself $5.50 a day will yield you $430,000 in 40 years (at a 7% return). That's all it takes. Think how much you would have if you saved $10, $20 or $30 a day! It is interesting to note that one of the largest categories of millionaires in the country is educators. As a group they do not make unusually high salaries but they make good savings and investment decisions. The earlier you begin to save the more money you will have in your nest egg when you choose not to work or can't work. Start early; look for base hits (conservative investments), not home runs (investments that promise a high rate of return with little risk which is unrealistic and usually deceitful). Go to bat often, save something of whatever you can and begin early. There are many investment opportunities. Select carefully. Be conservative and be consistent.

I know that for many young people thinking about retirement may seem a bit ridiculous. However, it is never too early to think about retirement. I often hear people of any age say, "I don't ever want to retire. I love my work." That may be but what if they cannot perform their work due to physical or mental problems? What then? How will they live the lifestyle they attained during the production phase of their life?

You don't have to command a high salary to acquire the ability to live well during retirement. You just have to have a plan.

I recently met a retired person who retired with two pensions and sizable investment money as well. He worked for a railroad company as a brakeman for twenty years and drove a bus for another twenty years and he and his wife invested a good portion of their salaries as well. I met him while we were camping. He owned a very nice motor home and owned two homes as well. He told me the pensions paid for all his living expenses. He is an example of doing well because he had a plan and not because he earned so much money during the production phase of his life.

Write briefly why the Financial Component is important for you.

_____

_____

_____

_____

_____

_____

COMMENTS: It is often said that money isn't important. Money cannot buy happiness or health. But is this true? When my mom would say to my dad that money cannot make you happy he would answer by saying that if he was going to be miserable he'd rather be rich and miserable than poor and miserable. Good point. And money can buy health to some extent because money can pay for treatment not otherwise covered by insurance. It is important to note that having more money doesn't make you a better person but it does afford you more choices. And if you are going to work why not make as much money doing what you like as long as it is moral, ethical and legal?

SPIRITUAL

The Spiritual Component of you includes those things that are not encompassed in the other components. It includes those things that are more emotional and emotive. It includes how you feel about life in general, your relationship to the universe, to a Supreme Being or the connectedness of all things. It is in this component that you will develop your belief system including the meaning of life, God, how you got here and why and your belief in an afterlife. Many feel they don't have time to develop the Spiritual Component of their being. Whether you realize it or not you have a spiritual self. The choice is, do you want to be in the driver's seat and direct this Component or sit in the back seat and let others do it for you? Participating in this Component of your life may not make you a better person, although hopefully it would, but it will make the journey more interesting and fulfilling. Your spiritual journey has less to do with an afterlife (if one exists) or going to church (which is OK, too) than making your journey in all its aspects here on earth more fulfilling.

Your spiritual life gives roots to your values. It gives stability to your life. It is your essence. It is what gives you a sense of right and wrong. Having a strong active spiritual life is what keeps you grounded. It helps you to develop an internal rather than an external reward system. You do the right thing because it is the right thing to do, not because it is what others expect. It is one of the reasons why people go to church to reinforce and feed the Spiritual Component of their being.

Write a few sentences describing what the Spiritual Component means to you.

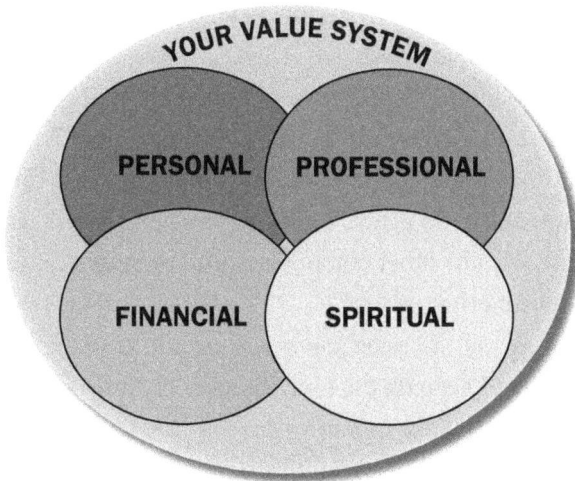

_____

_____

_____

_____

_____

Figure 3

Figure 3 shows how these four components work. It shows them as being separate but interrelated. The fifth circle represents your value system which is trying to compress those four circles so they are concentric. What affects one of the components affects the others as well. Sometimes it is said that some individuals are able to compartmentalize their behavior. This is often said to make an excuse for one who behaves poorly in one area as though that area of behavior is independent of the others. For example, an individual might value integrity and honesty but be in need of money so s/he becomes a drug dealer to satisfy his/her financial need. This would create an internal conflict between the Financial Component and the Spiritual, Personal and Professional Components of his/her being. S/he might seem OK to others as if nothing has changed, but that is just a facade. No matter how normal or effective s/he might look, s/he would know that what they are doing is not right and those four components would not be in alignment. Just like one wheel on a car being badly out of alignment will shake the whole car, that one component of your being out of alignment will affect your whole being. No matter how this person might pretend to be fine their internal conflict will cause suffering.

Another example might be an individual who wants to have some particular friends (the Personal Component). To gain their friendship may require compromising doing the right thing (Spiritual Component). So again, satisfying one component may cause misalignment in the other components and therefore cause internal conflict and suffering.

Figure 4 shows the outer circle representing your value system compressing and keeping the four components in alignment. If you satisfy the need to make money or have certain friends as in the examples above you will be in conflict with the Spiritual Component and you will be out of alignment. The outer circle, representing you, works to realign these components and therefore, you. In Figure 4 you can see that these four components are aligned within the larger circle. This is the goal throughout your life, keeping the four components of you aligned and in harmony with one another. This results in less stress; a feeling that all is well and that you are at peace and in harmony with yourself. This is the ideal but life isn't always ideal. You will likely find that you must take inventory of the four components periodically and realign if that is indicated.

Figure 4

Why is it important for you to understand the Four Components of your being?

_____

_____

_____

_____

_____

_____

_____

JASON HORNING, Pastor:

Spirituality for me is the center of who I am. My relationship with Jesus Christ has provided me with freedom from the guilt of sin and confidence that I have an eternal destiny with my Heavenly Father. Through my relationship with Jesus I have received the indwelling of the Holy Spirit who leads me each day, empowers me for the work God has called me to and gives me the strength to overcome sin. If my life could be looked at as a bike wheel, spirituality, or my relationship with Jesus, is the hub of the wheel. When Jesus is not the center of my life everything else I do is out of alignment. I keep Jesus at the center of my life by enjoying fellowship with Him daily through prayer.

Personally, I begin each day with an hour or two of worship, prayer and Scripture reading. Following this time I wake my wife up with a cup of coffee and we take a few minutes to read the Bible and pray together. Starting my day in this way has helped me keep Jesus at the center of my life and my wife close to my side. My relationship with Jesus has also greatly affected how I raise my children. I truly believe that the peace I have in my spirit enables me to be more loving, patient and understanding with my children. I also believe that the Bible gives indispensable instruction for raising my children in discerning right and wrong and understanding that there is a purpose for their existence. Professionally, I have the privilege of sharing my spirituality with others as my vocation. As a pastor I have the responsibility to study God's Word, pray and prepare messages that will help others grow spiritually. I also get to meet with people throughout the week and encourage them in their spiritual journey. Financially, I understand that everything I have is a gift from God. With this basic understanding I do my best to use the gifts I have been given wisely. My wife and I strive to avoid going into debt and spend only what we can afford. We are also intentional about putting money into savings for retirement and college funds for our children. We also try to give to others as much as possible and tithe 10% of what we make to the church.

Spirituality for me is not about rules or religion. Spiritually transcends every area of my life. It truly is a relationship that will never end.

ED ORLOSKY, High School Teacher (Retired):

I'm at peace with the four components of me. I strive to do the right thing and although I have made mistakes but, in general,

I believe I have led a life I am proud of. It is difficult to separate the four components as what affects one component affects them all. I have a good marriage, tried to do the best I could as a teacher. I was frugal and managed to take care of my financial component. I am fortunate to be able to be in a financial position to do whatever I want to do within reason.

I have tried to live by a code of conduct that respects others for what they believe. I have a set of moral values that values human respect and rights, compassion for others. I believe in promoting the common good of humanity. I have my individual wants and needs but in satisfying them I try to make sure they are satisfied in sync with what is good for everyone.

My spiritual component is more in line with mother-nature. The greatest gift is the gift of life. When I get up in the morning I know the best thing has already happened. The second best thing is knowing my wife is there with me.

COMMENTS: It seems to me that all you are and all you do fit into one or more of the components above. It would be fine if you decided to add a category or two. The point is to understand that all of these categories are part of you; they are one and the same. Just as we did in the Four Phases of Life, we separate them for ease of talking about them. We separate them so we can be specific in describing and understanding ourselves.

~Chapter 3~

Guidelines of Life

The following are a few guidelines to assist you in your life's journey. If these guidelines may seem simple it's because they are. In fact, you may think these guidelines may seem so simple that everyone would know them and implement them. But in my experience that has not been the case. Knowing them and implementing them are two very different things. Implementing them isn't easy but implementing them will help you to be more successful in every stage of your life, whether it is during grade school, high school, college, professional school or any other situation. So here are the guidelines of life.

SHOW UP
BE PRESENT
TELL THE TRUTH
LET GO OF OUTCOMES
LIGHTEN UP

SHOW UP

There will be many times when an opportunity arises and all you have to do is show up and take advantage of it. This opportunity might be a lecture, seminar, demonstration or training but it will require you to overcome inertia and get moving. If you just show up you will be ahead of many. You'll be pleasantly surprised at the advantage you will have gained by simply showing up. You might actually learn something that could help you in your life's journey. You might meet someone who has a need you might be able to help them achieve. You may also have an opportunity to find out what others want, helping them get what they want and helping yourself in this process. This is how the process of networking works; it creates symbiotic associations with others. If you show up and are open you will be able to take advantage of the power of networking. No matter what you have to do will take your effort but you can't do it alone, you will need help. Facilitate your achievements by using the multiplying power of networking. Networking will make your life a lot easier.

How could just "Showing Up" help you?

_____

_____

_____

_____

_____

_____

JOSIAH, age 8:

By biking to school I was able to "show up" and learn.

ALEX, age 13:

By showing up I could learn new things that help me be successful in life.

BE PRESENT

This is another way of saying wherever you are be all there, pay attention. Wherever you are, you're there anyway so why not make the best of it. In fact, someone once said, wherever you are that's where you'd rather be than any other place. That's because if you'd rather be someplace else you'd probably be there.

This guideline might seem easy but it really isn't. No matter where some people are they are often thinking of being or doing something else. Some seem to have mastered the art of always needing to be someplace else. Even when you are talking to someone they might seem to be hearing you, but they may not be listening. They're thinking of what they want to say to you or looking around to see if there is someone of greater interest to them. Or they might be texting and losing out on what could be an interesting or valuable opportunity.

A good exercise to determine if you were paying attention to what someone was saying is to say, "Let me see if I understand what you are saying," and then restate what you think you've heard and ask if you're correct. Steven Covey said, "Seek first to understand before seeking to be understood." Good things happen to those who are effective listeners. Listening to someone will help you to understand what they want. If you are interested in helping others, knowing what they want is the first step in helping them. Effective listeners earn more, learn more, and get better jobs than those who are not effective listeners.

You may be in a class you consider boring, listening to a dull speaker, or attending a meeting that seems like a waste of time. The fact is, you're there anyway. Make the most of it. There's a reason why you're sitting in the audience and not up in front of everyone and there is always something to learn. You might even think about what you could do if you were the presenter to make the class more interesting. You might think about how to be a more dynamic speaker or how to run a meeting more effectively and efficiently. How many opportunities are missed because someone is physically present but somewhere else mentally? Texting is a good example of being present physically but being somewhere else mentally. Paying attention and staying focused is a behavior that will yield huge returns for you.

How could "Being Present" help you?

_____

_____

_____

_____

_____

_____

_____

LAYLA, age 6:

At school I didn't know some of the words like 'the' and 'are' but I learned them by being present.

ALEX, age 13:

If you pay attention you can achieve more. If you focus, you may learn new things.

COMMENTS: I was attending Catholic school in 7th grade. During social studies the teacher would ask questions related to what was just read. It might be, "What is the principal industry of Canada?" Or, "What country borders the United States on the south?"

I thought it would be fun to take advantage of the situation. Some of the students (all boys), didn't pay attention, that is they "were not being present." When someone close to me was called upon, it was required for them to stand and answer the question. If they weren't paying attention, I would give them the answer. But the suggested answer was not always the correct one. Once the question was, "What is the capital of New York?" How easy was that question? But the student being asked was not being present, meaning he was not paying attention. I gave this student the answer ... "cattle." It made for a good laugh but at the expense of the answering student. I also had to run home for a few days after that one.

TELL THE TRUTH

Telling the truth is not always easy, especially if it requires you to admit you were wrong or that you have responsibility for something bad that happened. As difficult as that might be, it's easier to tell the truth and not have to make up stories you know aren't true. First of all it isn't right and secondly you'll have to remember what lie you told to whom. And thirdly you will almost always get caught anyway.

In Shakespeare's play *Hamlet*, Polonius gives advice to his son Laertes who is leaving home saying, "This above all; to thine own self be true, and it must follow, as night the day, thou canst not then be false to any man." Honesty is almost always the best policy but there are some other factors to consider.

There was an essay contest where anyone who entered had to write on the same topic. One year the topic was *Honesty is the Best Policy*, and it was won by a Catholic priest who said that honesty is not always the best policy. He gave an example of years ago in Germany when the Nazis were in search of Jews to send to the concentration camps. Some non-Jews were hiding Jews. When asked by the Nazis if they had seen any Jews many would answer, "No." Not the truth, but a better choice considering that particular situation. Of course this is an unusual situation. The point here is, think of the consequences and the greater good before you speak.

Telling the truth is important. But I wouldn't be telling the truth if I didn't admit we all lie in some situations and that it might be better to lie than to tell the truth. Suppose you did something nice for someone in need. You refuse their offer to pay you money. To thank you they bring you some homemade ginger snap cookies. You have an intense dislike for ginger snap cookies. Do you tell them that? Of course not. You might say something like, "This is very nice of you. Certainly unexpected, but not unappreciated." And then hope they don't reward you in the same manner in the future.

Being honest doesn't mean you have to be hurtful. You can say what you need to say in a kind and considerate manner. And before you say anything, consider if saying it is necessary at all. Ben Franklin said, "A slip of the foot you may soon recover, but a slip of the tongue you may never get over."

What are the challenges you face in telling the truth?

_____

_____

_____

_____

_____

_____

_____

LEAH, Age 6:

It is hard to tell the truth each and every day but I feel bad when I lie.

ELLIE, Age 10:

One time I said I did all 10 pages of my homework and played video games instead of doing my homework. The next day I was getting ready for school and my mom checked to see if I had my homework. My mom asked why I didn't get my homework done. I felt guilty and anxious about going to school. I learned not to procrastinate and get my work done before I play.

LET GO OF THE OUTCOME

In certain situations we all have what we believe to be great ideas. We may communicate these ideas only to find that others do not have the same opinion that we do. How is this possible? It is such a good idea. Well, that's life. What we consider to be a "no brainer" others may see as not very worthy. It is usually a blow to our ego. We are best served by moving on, letting go, being at peace with the situation. We made a suggestion and it was not well received. At least we tried. If that is the worst thing that happens to us we will be fortunate indeed!

Occasionally a parent or grandparent will observe their children or grandchildren doing something that might not be in their best interest. They may offer a suggestion but the child or grandchild may do what they want to anyway. This may cause some parents or grandparents to wonder why they were unable to influence their child or grandchild to do things the way they think it should be done. It is not always easy to let go of the outcome. It takes continual practice. But the payoff is peace of mind.

When I was working and would visit a satellite clinic often an employee would come to me and say, "Bob, can I speak to you alone for a few minutes?" When that happened they wanted to talk to me about changing the behavior of another person. For example, one person said, "I know I'm getting paid the same as so and so, however, they leave work an hour before me every day." Upon questioning I found out that the person who leaves early dictates their notes over lunch hour. But the person who was talking to me did not want to do that. They felt they needed the time to relax over lunch hour. But they still wanted to leave work the same time as the person who chose to write their notes over their lunch hour.

In the above examples the person did not get what they wanted because they were trying to control the behavior of another person. Parents and grandparents usually learn that their children or grandchildren have their own minds and behave in the way they deem appropriate. Employees cannot control the behavior of their co-workers.

Both of the above cases were an attempt by someone to change the behavior or thought process of another person. The only person you can change is yourself and that's not as easy as it sounds. If it were there would be no criminals; society would be perfect and we would have no need for psychiatry, psychologists or social workers.

There is a prayer called the Serenity Prayer which is as follows:

> God, grant me the serenity to accept the things I cannot change,
> Courage to change the things I can,
> And the wisdom to know the difference.

This prayer does not mean that you don't offer suggestions and that you don't attempt to affect change for the better. What it does mean is after you try, let go of the outcome. You have no control over it. Feeling serenity in that situation means being at peace with yourself and not agonizing over the fact that what you wanted to change hasn't occurred. The courage to change the things that you can relates to changing your own thoughts and behavior. As I mentioned previously, that's not particularly easy but all you can control is yourself. Make your suggestion but if you are not successful, let go of the outcome.

Nini and I have participated in Search and Rescue for quite a while. There are members who are known as paramedics. A few of these paramedics complain about how physicians with whom they work are inadequate. They believe they know more about emergency medicine than the doctors. This may be true but they're forgetting the reality of the situation. That is, they are not doctors and the doctor is the one who determines the course of treatment. If they really want to control things, they should go to medical school and become a doctor themselves (and then some paramedics will complain about them). But for a variety of reasons, this may be too difficult so they may continue complaining and feeling frustrated. What they really need to do is let go of the outcome.

How can this section help you to Let Go of the Outcome?

_____

_____

_____

_____

_____

_____

_____

MAYA, age 10:

One time when my friend and his younger sister came over, I wanted to play outside and have a water fight because it was a hot summer day. My friend's sister doesn't like water fights, so we had to find something else we could do together. I was a little frustrated because I really wanted to have a water fight,

30

but I finally got over it and realized that if I stayed frustrated we wouldn't have any fun. So we did something else where we would all be happy and have fun. And we did. I learned that it is better to let your outcomes roll off smoothly than to stay frustrated and off on your own.

COMMENTS: A very difficult thing for a parent is to know when to let your children make their own mistakes. Sometimes children won't listen to their parents even when what their parents say is correct. It is difficult because parents love their children and would like them to progress through life without getting hurt. When a child is hurt the parent is hurt as well. This is where letting go is usually best for the parent and child as well. Parents have to coach themselves to let go of the outcome as it relates to their children. It is not easy for parents to emotionally accept and believe that they cannot take the responsibility for their children's failures but they cannot take credit for their successes either.

LIGHTEN UP

There will be times when you think you have a great idea. You might think others should embrace it enthusiastically only to see it rejected. This is not an easy thing to deal with. Rejection always hurts, but it will happen and when it does, it helps not to take yourself too seriously. There's a little book that's entitled, *Don't Sweat the Small Stuff* by Richard Carlson. The subtitle is, *And it's all small stuff.* In other words, make your point (or case), let go of the outcome, and feel good about what you did. Life is short, don't agonize over things, and lighten up.

Give examples of how the "Lighten Up" guideline could be useful to you.

_____

_____

_____

_____

_____

_____

_____

AL SLAVIN, Self Storage Owner:

In my daily business life I realize that life happens to my customers. Some may be dealing with unfortunate circumstances. So they may be unable to pay their storage unit rental. I try to accommodate their needs but sometimes I have no choice but to auction the contents of their storage unit. Even after 15 years it still breaks my heart to do this but I have no choice if I want to remain in business.

Lightening up keeps me sane. I try to prioritize what's important. Things that have the potential to cause me to not be able to lighten up or laugh aren't worth perseverating over. I replace it with something that puts a smile on my face such as making a nice dinner, going for a workout, watching a movie, *looking at the sky or being excited to see my wife when she comes home from work.*

When I compare myself to others I wouldn't trade with anyone. I'm thankful for the ride I'm on. How fortunate I am. I always try to accentuate the positive.

JEAN MacARTHUR, M.S., U.S. Air Force Lt Col (retired):

Occasionally, just showing up may result in good things happening. My husband and I have been in situations where it may have been easier to stay at home and not go out. We have gone to some plays whose subject matter I thought might have been too heavy to enjoy. This has resulted in interesting conversations that lasted far longer than the play.

Being present or focusing on the moment is not always easy. Not thinking about the past or what I have to do in the future takes effort. But it is worth the effort. All we know we have is the present. We may as well enjoy it.

Telling the truth is almost always the best thing to do. It makes it easier to interact with others. Telling the truth makes it easier to remember what you said. But it is not always easy either. It's nice to be honest but in some areas telling a little white lie in a social situation so as not to hurt someone else's feelings might be the better choice. When someone says, "How do I look?" (especially if it's your spouse) you always say, "You look terrific to me!" even if she or he looks like they just got out of bed.

Sometimes we put too much emphasis on winning or losing. I always had goals. These goals have changed as I have moved through life. Some of my goals I have achieved, others were modified or deleted from my life. Sometimes it was necessary to just let go of the outcome. It always feels better to win than to lose but if we did our best shouldn't that be satisfying in itself? Maybe we could reframe our efforts into developing a win-win solution to a problem or situation. But when we have given it our best try and came up short, it is good to let go of the outcome. Life will go on.

We don't laugh enough. I was blowing snow today and the wind was blowing the snow back on the drive as fast as I was removing it. My neighbor saw this and laughed. I saw him laughing and began to laugh myself. I am able to laugh at myself and not let what others think interfere with my having a good time.

COMMENTS: I was giving a talk while hosting a picnic for my company. I was making what I thought was an important point. I raised my hand and came down with what I thought would be a slap on the table for emphasis. I missed the table but did not miss upsetting the salad bowl. I sent the salad complete with salad dressing all over my front including my face. As embarrassed as I was, we all had a good laugh over my mistake. My ego was momentarily deflated but it wasn't a big deal and the company and I survived because I was able to lighten up.

~Chapter 4~

Civility

Our society, or any society, requires civility to function well. Civility means being polite, courteous and respectful. Civility makes it easier and less stressful to interact with one another. "Civility costs nothing, and buys everything" (Mary Wortley Montagu).

"Civility means a great deal more than just being nice to one another. It is complex and encompasses learning how to connect successfully and live well with others, developing thoughtfulness, and fostering effective self-expression and communication. Civility includes courtesy, politeness, mutual respect, fairness, good manners, as well as a matter of good health." (Pier Massimo Forni).

Manners are an important part of civility. Manners are acceptable ways of behaving in any given social situation. Good manners show respect for anyone with whom you are interacting. It provides an understanding of what to expect from those engaged in a social or business interaction. Observing good manners makes any social occurrence more predictable and less stressful. George Washington said, "Every action done in company ought to be with some sign of respect to those that are present."

When I was growing up I was told, "Children should be seen and not heard." In the presence of adults, children should not speak unless spoken to. Children were expected to say "Pleased to meet you" or "How do you do" whenever introduced to someone. Children were told to "mind your Ps and Qs." That meant to always say please and thank you. Elders were addressed as Mr. or Mrs. and "yes sir, no sir" was an appropriate response. This was the norm during my formative years. These required behaviors were part of the social behavior code that was expected to be observed. Not observing these rules resulted in a swift reaction from parents. Often this meant receiving some sort of corporal punishment. We also learned about manners in school. We were taught how to write letters of introduction, thank you letters and how to fold and place letters in envelopes. We lived in an adult-centered world and we were considered to be in training to become productive adults.

Both my parents were employed outside the home. I was expected to go to my dad's barber shop after school. I did this until I was in seventh grade. I will always remember my dad addressing his customers and anyone else as "sir" or "ma'am" even if he knew their names. I remember being somewhat embarrassed by this. I thought it was being subservient. It was only later that I realized this demonstrated respect for those with whom he interacted. I remember his shop was almost always filled and that his customers seemed to enjoy being there. And why not, he made them feel special.

Today, we seemed to have become a child-centered world. Parents negotiate with their children for just about everything from when to do homework, chores, where to go on vacation, etc. I have heard children address each other and even adults as "Dude." How disrespectful. Have some respect and address people by their names. Even though parents seem to be more tolerant of the behavior exhibited by their children it is still a world ruled by adults. When children become adults will addressing their boss as "Dude" be beneficial? This transition would be made easier if civility became the cornerstone of your behavior.

Civility does not mean there is an absence of questioning or analysis of what was read or heard. It means that it is done in a manner that is respectful of others. It encourages a civil discussion and values the opinions of others. Maya Angelou said it well in the following quote: "I've learned that people will forget what you said, people will forget what you did, but people will never forget how you made them feel."

So, watch your Ps and Qs (please and thank you), be polite, considerate, respectful and kind. Say thank you a lot. Being considerate and displaying good manners will make others feel better for having interacted with you and good things will come your way.

Why is it important to be civil?

_____

_____

_____

_____

_____

GEMMA, age 8:

One time, I was playing with my friend who is a little bossy. When it was time for her to go, she started yelling at her mom and throwing a fit. It made me feel uncomfortable and I felt bad for her mom. I learned that when children behave badly and don't have any manners, adults and sometimes kids don't want to be around them.

LAYLA, age 8:

Once I had to go to school and I had to learn my manners because I want to be kind, honest and respectful to my teacher and other students. And manners make me represent my family well.

ROB, age 16, High School Sophomore:

In my high school I try to keep things on a regular friendly basis. I might say, "Hi Dude" to someone, maybe not as respectful as calling them by name. This is a familiar way for me to greet a friend. It's like saying 'it's good to see you or hi friend.' It is a casual greeting. But I realize that grownups might feel comfortable with a more courteous greeting.

I learned at an early age to treat others with respect and realize how I communicate with my peers is not the way to communicate with adults and with my teachers. Teachers seem to like students who show them respect and are polite. This is the best way I know to develop a comfort level between myself and my teachers.

I try to make my education be a true learning situation every day and not just another day. Every day brings opportunities to learn and being civil is a great way to establish relationships with those who may be able to help me determine the right path for my life.

BETTY BENSON, Mayor Pro-Tem, County Public Information Officer:

I think a good lesson in manners and civility would be easily viewed in the TV series 'Downton Abbey.' Old England, castle life, and the way they treated each other as well as those in their communities provides a great visual.

Our society doesn't really give us such a view. We no longer care which fork we eat with, whether the spoon and knife goes on the left or the right, do I really need to write a thank-you note for this gift I received from Grandma. Do I really need to ask that person over for dinner because they invited me to dinner, can I slurp my soup and let it run down my chin while eating with others, and can't I burp or fart in public and not have to say excuse me? *Of course you can do all of these things, but what outcome do you hope to achieve by not being polite?*

But the real value of manners or civility lies in how we treat each other day in and day out. Certainly I have the right to be rude, offensive to others, show my disdain of another and in general just live my life as it suits me without regard to anyone else.

I keep my yard neat and tidy — not just because it looks nice, but it is not offensive to my neighbors. I don't sit in public and swear, or make out with another person, or be so loud as to be disruptive to those around me. Do I have the right to do those things? Sure. Do I really need to do them? Probably not. Is there a benefit to not doing them? I believe there is.

It was probably easier to be civil, show manners, when the population was smaller, and perhaps less invasive in our personal space. But it is where we are and being aware of the circumstances of others can still take our society a long ways.

COMMENTS: When I was growing up I thought my parents were too concerned about being civil and behaving appropriately. But they were right to do so. It helped me to get along with people of different ages and walks of life. If life were a game, civility would be one of the most important rules.

~Chapter 5~

CHOICES

Everything you do is a choice that you make. And the choices you make determine the quality of your life. I expect you think you already know this and perhaps you do, but understanding it and implementing it are very different things. Someone a lot smarter than me said, "Human beings through thought alone have the ability to change the very fabric of their life for the better and then choose to do the opposite." This surely seems to be the rule in our society today. I look at so many people who seem to be struggling and seem to be less successful than they would like to be. They don't seem to understand the choices that they've made have put them where they are and choices that they may make could help them to better themselves.

Everything you do is a choice you make. Everything! Obeying your parents, going to school, the games you play, how you treat your siblings, doing your homework and the quality of the work you do are all choices you make. Your parents don't have to pay the electric bill, the mortgage or buy groceries. They choose to do these things. But of course the choices you make have consequences in your life. If you choose not to obey your parents, you might get punished. If you don't go to school you might not learn valuable information that might make it easier for you as you go through kindergarten through 12th, college, trade school, etc. You and only you can decide how you will behave. It's not always easy, your emotions may say, "Go ahead, do it, punch him. It will feel good to do it," and actually it might for a brief period of time. Your logical mind says, "If you do it you'll get punished." It's still a choice; you will have to decide what you will do and you'll have to deal with the consequences.

If your parents decide not to pay the electric bill the energy company may shut off power to your home. No TV, no video games, no lights or other conveniences. If they don't pay the mortgage, they might become homeless and you along with them. They choose to pay these things in order to have electricity, a nice place to live and other conveniences. That's a choice they make. These and other choices you make determine the quality of your life. Do you want to be happy, enjoy school and work and be well off financially? These are dependent upon the choices that you make as you go through life.

It is said that 5% of people make things happen, 15% of people watch things happen and 80% wonder what happened. In which group you find yourself is the result of the choices you make. Whether you read this or not, or implement what you read or not, is a choice you will make. I hope you'll make the best choice for you. Someone once said to me that life is a game. If it is a game, knowing the rules makes playing the game easier and more successful for the player. What is contained in this book are some of the rules of this game of life.

Everyone is born, dies and something happens in-between. Much of what happens is due to the choices you make. Some things that happen to you are not of your choosing, but even in this case you can choose how you will either respond or react. It is said, "It is not what happens to you that matters but what you do with what happens to you that counts." So it's still about choices.

Even your attitude is a choice that you make. Not many people enjoy thinking of their death, but it's going to happen. It happens to everyone, it will happen to you. You just don't know when. In dealing with this reality you can greet each new day and get up and realize you're one day closer to your death. Or, you could wake, take a deep breath, and rejoice in the fact that you are alive. Enjoy the moment because it's all you have.

I had a friend by the name of Leonard. He wasn't gifted intellectually and his nickname was "Crazy," not very flattering. Every time we ran together, Leonard would tell me it was the best run of his life. After hearing him say this so many times I could no longer ignore it and had to ask, "How is it that every run is the best run of your life, surely there were some better runs. Maybe they were easier, more scenic, something that would make one run better than another." Leonard's response was, "Well I can't bring back yesterday. Tomorrow might not come. That makes this the best run of my life." How wise…Leonard may not have been intellectually gifted but he was a very wise man. He is one of my heroes.

So how you go through life is up to you, it's your choice. Here's an algorithm that might be useful to you.

If you like it, enjoy it.
If you don't like it, change it.
If you cannot change it, avoid it.
If you cannot avoid it, change your attitude.

Someone asked me what I thought was the meaning of life. I answered, "It is whatever you want it to be." I may be wrong, but I believe we have a free will and the ability to choose our destiny. It may be true that some people are successful in life because they are destined to. But most succeed because they are determined to. I hope you will be determined to be successful.

List techniques you might employ to assure you will make the best Choices for you.

_____

_____

_____

_____

_____

_____

_____

KEIRA, age 8:

A few days ago I didn't do my homework. I played outside instead. Then I forgot about it and had to get up early in the morning so I could get it done. I learned it is better to do my homework first and then go out to play.

CHOICES

LAYAH, age 8:

Once in my class we were in math and my class got out of control. We were running, screaming and not listening. I decided to do the right thing. I chose to listen and show respect to my teacher because it was the right thing to do.

MAYA, age 10:

There were some girls at school I wanted to be friends with. They made fun of some other girls who were fat. I knew that wasn't right so even though I wanted to be in their group of friends, I decided it wasn't the right thing to do.

YAKOV, age 10:

You always have choices that can be hard to choose. The first way to make a good choice is to look at all the choices as the best and the worst. The second is to decide yourself and that it is your choice and nobody can decide for you. The last is that you should be positive about your choices and not brag to other people about your choices.

RYAN FITZMAURICE, Newspaper Reporter:

Who you are is defined by the choices you make. Every choice defines you. The person you are at any given moment is formed by the decisions you're making. That makes a human being a shifting irregular thing. We don't often make our choices on any easily deciphered continuum, and even the best person can make the worst choices. So, I'm saying two things here. The first is that you will not escape bad choices, but they are also not a failure. They are a part of life, and they are a part of you. They will allow you to grow. As an individual who was often debilitated by social anxiety, ordering a pizza on the phone was already what seemed an insurmountable challenge, so asking uncomfortable questions to strangers who didn't really want to talk to me in the first place was especially never going to happen. So, of course, when I joined my college newspaper, it was to write music reviews, and absolutely not to partake in journalism. That didn't happen. My editor, who I will always have gratitude for, decided to ignore my requests and gave me an assignment, it was just a bowling party, but I was terrified.

That's how my love for journalism began. I had faced something which made me deeply uncomfortable, that challenged me profoundly, and I had overcome it. I found myself enthralled by that. Within a year, I had won a state-wide award, and gained an internship. And within only a few months after graduating college, I had fulfilled a dream. I was writing for a living. It was all because I made the choice not to be comfortable and to do something which frightened me. The fulfillment I get from journalism doesn't come because it is easy, but rather because it is hard.

The second observation is this: Who you are and what you want to become is entirely up to you. Any ideal you have for who you want to be is not out of reach. Know who that person is, make the choices that person will make, and you quite literally are that person. I think most of us form some distinction about who we are on the inside and who we are on the outside as if they're two separate entities. The person inside you is "the real you" while the person people see is some imperfect reflection. I would like to challenge that notion. Surely, as you grow older you will hear many things about how we are a product of our environment and our past. I do not dispute these things, nor ignore the profound indications of them. But I also believe what separates us from the other species on this planet is we have agency. We can be rational. We can make choices independent from our biology and conditioning. That means you are free. It may be the most terrifying and incredible thing you could ever ask for. Cherish that decision, never forget. Let your freedom define you more than anything else.

COMMENTS: Everything you do is a choice and the choices you make determine the quality of your life. As simple as this is it is difficult to understand why so many people choose to ignore this principle. I am always troubled by the young people I see smoking, displaying tattoos and multiple pierced body parts from which ornaments are hanging. Rarely do these things help them get a job or learn a marketable skill. These things do not help them to develop a successful life. These choices seem to say to me, "I don't feel good about myself. I want to be appreciated and noticed." Get noticed they will but generally not in a positive manner. They may understand the principle above but understanding and application are very different things.

∽Chapter 6∽

RISK AND REWARD

You will undoubtedly hear people talk about risk and reward. What they mean is that just about everything you do has some risk associated with it. Deciding to actually do the activity in question is always determined by the risk relative to the reward. If the risk is great and the reward is small the activity might not seem worthwhile. On the other hand, if the reward is perceived to be greater than the risk, the activity may be perceived as being worthwhile. In general, the greater the perceived or actual risk associated with an activity, the greater the perceived or actual reward.

It was a risk to your wellbeing when you learned to walk. You could fall, and you did, many times. But the reward in terms of your increased mobility made it worthwhile. The same is true when you learned to ride a two wheeled bike. You crashed many times, occasionally getting banged up in the process. But once you learned how to handle the bike it was worth the bruises you may have experienced. Now your world greatly expanded. This is true of just about anything you do. Skiing, hiking, camping, backpacking, playing a musical instrument, the course of study you choose all are associated with risk and reward.

Evaluating risk and reward will be present your entire life. In the Educational Phase of your life you will make choices about what courses to take. The course of study you choose has a risk and a reward associated with it. You might learn more in a difficult class but it will be more difficult to achieve a good grade. Usually, a difficult educational pathway is a greater risk but it is also associated with a greater reward. Fewer people choose the difficult educational path. Because there are fewer of them, replacing them would be difficult and therefore they are more valuable. It is not easy taking a risk because you could fail. But as someone once said, "You miss 100% of the shots you don't take."

If you think about it everything you do has risk associated with it. Every medication has a benefit, that is why you consider taking it. It also has side effects that are not beneficial. Even aspirin can cause stomach problems or a decrease in white blood cell count, neither of which are good. You weigh the risks of taking (or not taking) the aspirin and make your decision accordingly. You always consider the potential risks associated with anything you do and weigh them against the potential rewards. Most reasonable people look at BASE jumping (jumping off buildings, antennas, spans of earth) and decide the risk (death) is not worth the thrill of jumping off one of the BASE objects. But others will conclude it is worth the risk. I think they need to have their heads examined! You will want to take risks but you will need to calculate the reward associated with the particular risk. The reward might make taking the risk worthwhile.

I found a brief statement attributed to author Rabbi Harold Kushner that I thought appropriate.

Choosing a no risk lifestyle is, in itself, a tragic risk. We become emotionally anesthetized. We learn to live our whole life within narrow emotional range, accepting the fact there will be few high spots in exchange for the guarantee, there will be one gray day after another.

This next poem by Janet Rand I thought worth reprinting here as well.

To laugh is to risk appearing the fool,
To weep is to risk being called sentimental.
To reach out to another is to risk involvement.
To expose feelings is to risk showing your true self.
To place your ideas and your dreams before the crowd is to
risk being called naive.
To love is to risk not being loved in return,
To live is to risk dying,
To hope is to risk despair.
To try is to risk failure

But risks must be taken, because the greatest risk in life is to risk nothing. For the person who risks nothing, does nothing, has nothing, is nothing and becomes nothing. Chained to his certitude, he is a slave; he has forfeited his freedom. Only the person who risks is truly free.

Write several ways Risk and Reward may be present in your life now and in your immediate future.

_____

_____

_____

_____

_____

_____

_____

YAKOV age 10:

Sometime you have to take risks but before you do that you have to estimate the effect. Will you be rewarded or will it be worse? OK, so look at it like this. If you go skiing and are about to jump off a cliff will this reward you and you will get high fives from your friends and learn from it or will you get badly hurt? Take risks but not too big.

WENDY WYMAN, Superintendent of Schools:

I had a lot of great experiences in my previous background as a principal. I had to interact with other principals, teachers and multiple stakeholders collaborating on many issues. It was a rewarding, positive and effective experience. When the *superintendent of schools decided to resign I thought I could bring my positive experiences I learned collaborating with others with me to this school system. The more one is able to be a leader the more fulfilling the position of superintendent and the more fulfilling the positions of all one works with becomes. Everyone is valued and has an opportunity to contribute and that contribution is appreciated. No one has a monopoly on good ideas. I appreciate the input of others and I believe others want to contribute as well. Working together we can all accomplish more than any one of us alone. That's why I applied for the position.*

But there were risks associated with applying. The school system was performing at a low level. Not an easy situation to turn around. I thought we could succeed but success was not guaranteed. We could fail but failing was not an option I would welcome. Additionally, the interview was much more public than I previously experienced. I tend to be a private, quiet person so putting myself in a position to be scrutinized by the public was a personal risk.

Obviously, I was chosen for the position. The risks were worth the reward. It is so exciting to be in a position where I can facilitate opportunities for our kids and staff. The community is really a great fit for me. I learn daily from others. I feel energized and it is not easy but I can see we are on the path to creating the environment I imagined. Taking risks is important to learning and experiencing new rewarding situations. You may not always get what you want but it is always better than not trying. You might feel as though you are falling off a cliff but it might just be a curb. A quote I remember is, 'You always miss 100% of the shots you don't take.'

COMMENTS: Everything you do will have some risks. When I was in high school it was important for every boy's self-esteem to make the varsity team (as opposed to junior varsity). Any team was good as long as it was varsity. But you had to try out for the team. Not everyone made the team. Some were "cut", that is told not to show up for additional practices, they didn't make the team. It was embarrassing if you got cut but it was worth the risk if you made the team. My advice is to take risks and make your life an adventure.

When I was going to college I was working at a convenience store. A driver for a delivery service came into the store and I discovered he made three times what I was being paid. I decided to apply for a truck driver's job. The driver told me they wouldn't hire a student. I decided to take the risk anyway. The next day I went to the delivery business's location and asked to see the owner of the business. I went into his office and told him I knew he needed to make a profit and that I would do my best to do what I could do to make that happen. He sent me to the foreman to take a driving test. I drove the truck around the yard. I was told to back the truck into the dock. There was a vertical post between the warehouse doors. Two trucks fit into the space between the vertical posts. So I drove around the yard and lined up the truck. I noticed the garage seemed to be very wide. I was backing up and *boom*, I backed into the post between the garage doors. I felt so stupid. I thought I would not get the job. But I did! It was fun and I made a good rate of pay. So, this time, taking the risk wasn't easy but the reward made it worth taking. It didn't always turn out this way but it did often enough that even though taking a risk (a calculated risk) is just that, a risk, it is worth taking. If I didn't take risks nothing would happen.

∼ Chapter 7 ∼

FORM AND ESSENCE

HOW DO YOU MEASURE YOUR SELF-WORTH, YOUR SELF-ESTEEM? WHO ARE YOU?

These questions might seem to have a simple answer. When someone asks you who you are you'll usually state your name. But does this really tell anyone who you are? It does tell them how you are known, how to separate you from others, except for those who have the same name. Who you are is really a complicated question because we are all complicated beings. Who you are is related not only to your family tree but also to your values, morals and beliefs. These are difficult to communicate to another person primarily for two reasons. The first is that communication is very difficult at best. You're attempting to get a thought from your mind and cause another person to understand your thoughts, many of which are abstract in nature.

The second is that most individuals won't take the time and effort to understand you and your thoughts. It is through understanding these facts and your own beliefs, values, morals and behavior that will help you to understand others. You might be inclined to say, "Who cares?" In this world, understanding others will make it easier for you to achieve your goals. We will talk about this later.

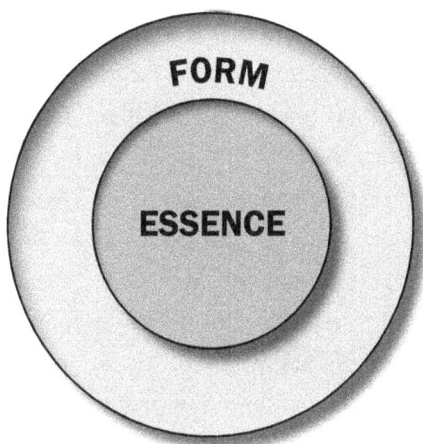

Figure 5

Now let's look at who you are. It is not possible for others to define or read your thoughts but it is possible to describe your behavior. Your behavior says something about who you think you are and how you value yourself. This is what is meant by self-esteem. There are two main ways to measure your self-esteem. In figure 5 there is an inner circle which represents your essence. In this circle are things that include your values and beliefs. It is who you are when you take away all of your material things. It is the essential or in-trinsic you. Being true to your essence is what will help you to avoid doing something you know not to be the right thing to do just be-cause a group with whom you want to associate thinks it should be done. The second area is a concentric circle drawn around the essence circle. It is larger and represents your form and consists of superficial things that we all have that also define who we are. These things might include who you value as friends, the clothes you wear, where you live, the toys you have and adults have toys too, such as cars, skis, cell phones, etc. It includes how you dress, the car you drive, where you live, the watch you wear and other outwardly visible things. What is important is not those things that make up your form but why you have chosen those things. Did you choose these things because you wanted to impress others or because you really wanted them regardless of what others thought? Or is it a combination of the two. Did you choose where you live to impress others? If you have a car, do you drive a car that is a small part of your discretionary income? Or do you drive a vehicle you can ill afford so that others will think you are well off financially. What is most important is not what you have, but why you have what you have.

Before you can afford to buy any of these things on your own, you may be asking Mom and Dad to foot the bill. It's important to ask yourself, "Why do I want these things?" Be introspective. Ask yourself, "How important are my possessions in measuring my self-worth?" Decide for yourself if you are trying to impress others or fill a personal need.

You might have heard it said you can't argue with yourself, but we all probably do this from time to time. For example, you might have a friend whose relationship you value (part of your form). This friend might ask you to do something you don't feel is right (which might negatively affect your essence). The argument is between your form and your essence. Do you do what your friend is asking you to do to maintain your friendship or do you decline to do what you believe is wrong to maintain your essence and integrity? Choices like this will happen often in your life. Choosing between the easy decision and the more difficult decision will not always be easy. The question is between building your form or your essence.

The point is each of us measures our self-esteem both internally and externally. We all measure our self-worth by both form and essence. The relative size of each is what matters. Do you think you are better off living your life and measuring your self-esteem from the outside in (form) or from the inside out (essence)? The relative size of your essence compared to your form determines the depth of your character.

This is true whether it is about choosing a political candidate to vote for, where you will go to school, how neatly you complete your homework or which job to accept.

Self-esteem and how it is measured is something that will affect you your entire life. The effect your self-esteem has on your behavior is obvious, but how others measure their own self-esteem will affect you as well. Let me give you a real life example . . . At one point in my life I worked for IBM. I received a promotion to a computing department. My job was to learn to run a particular computer. The chief operator of that computer was named Jenny. It was a long time ago and computers didn't get turned on simply by pushing the "on" button. One had to key in machine language into the machine to get it to function properly. Sometimes the code that was entered into the machine didn't turn it on. Jenny knew how to open a service panel, push some buttons and basically reset the machine so that it would work. The computer programmers who used the machine loved Jenny because she could always get the machine to function properly. I thought that this would be a good thing to know, so I asked Jenny if she would show me the particular codes that she entered into the customer service panel. She said I didn't need to know them.

This of course interfered with my ability to understand that machine as thoroughly as she did. But that was purposeful on her part. She wanted to maintain her level of importance on that machine. Not to be discouraged by Jenny's behavior, I asked some engineers what the codes were in the customer service panel. They told me and I learned how to use them. What Jenny did by not telling me and others those codes was to guarantee that she would be the preeminent operator on that particular computer. As it turned out, that computer was determined to be obsolete and along with it, Jenny. This was an example of how Jenny's behavior to maintain her self-esteem limited others (and her own) ability to be successful.

When faced with such a situation, it has helped me to ask the question, "Whose problem is it?" After determining whose problem it is, let them own it. If someone is nasty to you, don't take it personally. It may be because they don't feel particularly good about themselves. This is not to say that you should be a door mat for anyone else's behavior. They need to be held accountable for what they do, but even that can be done in a thoughtful, kind manner.

Someone who has good self-esteem knows that by helping others to do well they feel better about themselves. Those who do not have good self-esteem believe that by putting others down, their own level of self-esteem is increased, but the opposite is actually true. When you see someone putting down someone that is shorter than them, not as smart as they are, it tells you that they have poor self-esteem. But also remember, no one's self-esteem is so good that it couldn't stand a little improvement.

Both Form and Essence are measures of our self-esteem. What will you do to make sure you maintain the "right" proportion of each?

_____

_____

_____

_____

_____

_____

_____

ANNETTE ESQUEDA, age 19, Bookstore Manager and College Student majoring in Education:

I am a manager at Barnes and Noble bookstore and a college student. Essence is about knowing who you are. It is about feeling comfortable with yourself. I expect this will be a lifelong procedure. In my daily life I see those who in order to feel better about themselves need to have things like jewelry, clothes and cars to make a statement about who they are. We all need these things but form should not define who we are.

I believe we are like flowers, blossoming as we grow. Every situation is an opportunity for growth. The people I surround myself with are life's vessel. Their outlook, beliefs, attitude and *their journey have an effect on me. I try to surround myself with positive role models. I seek advice and counsel from these people. My parents, family and friends all provide examples of how I want to be, to develop my essence. These things pervade all aspects of my life and influence the clothes I wear, where I decide to go and even where I eat.*

I set goals for myself to stabilize my life and my essence. I try to have balance in all I do. Life is about defining who you are and growing those roots. Form is a necessary part of my life but essence is really what defines me as a person.

TRISH KING, Office Manager and Mom:

We owned a home in a neighborhood not far from town for a number of years. It was a bit small for our family but served us well. We sold that home and several months ago we moved to a new home, at least new to us. It is larger than our previous home and has beautiful views. And we purchased it at a very good price. We now have a home that is a very good investment that will be realized when we retire. And as added benefit, I have a "Wow, I can't believe this is ours!" feeling every time we come home and I walk in the door and see our beautiful home and the gorgeous views.

By definition where and how we live could be considered part of our form. You could say that this home, or any home for that matter, is part of our form. But we have to live somewhere and we love it here. It is part of the reason for working, to be able to choose where and how we live.

When we moved into our new home, we noticed our neighbors' expensive cars and their homes looked like they may have had decorators design them. They probably did. We needed more furniture and accessories to complete our home. This is also part of our form. But here is where our essence takes precedence over form. We have always lived below our means and will not change now. There are things we may want and need. Soon we will need a newer car. We will purchase what we can afford regardless of what the neighbors might think. We are not ones to "Keep up with the Joneses." Form and essence are both important. We need to have both. It is the relative importance you place on each that is important.

COMMENTS: Form and essence, self-esteem and integrity are closely linked. Here's a story of how some adults in a small community dealt with this issue. A tax supported public institution was in financial trouble and had been for many years. This institution was asking the voters to approve a large increase in property taxes to support the institution. But it was obvious that the need for the business didn't exist. It could never be self-supporting. It needed to change and without going into detail let me say this was obvious. In a public forum where some prominent residents were asked how they would vote it seemed to be a mutual admiration society. "Anyone in favor, raise your hand." At first no one raised their hand. Then one person had the courage to raise their hand. Seeing this, another raised their hand. Looking at one another, another hand raised and then another until just about everyone raised their hand. Voting against this would have been very unpopular even though each person individually probably realized the obvious and right choice was to vote no.

~Chapter 8~

VALUES, BELIEFS AND BEHAVIORS

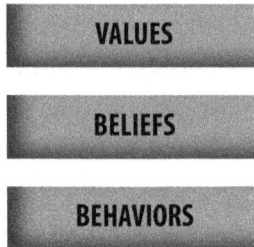

Figure 6

Values are those things you hold dear to yourself. They make you who you believe yourself to be. They include things such as honesty, compassion, empathy, work ethic and respect for yourself and others. Values can and do change. Some values are kept for a lifetime; others may be added or deleted. They are important because they are used to create our mental maps and guide our behavior. That's why you behave as you do.

I hope that a good work ethic is part of what you value. Your work ethic to a large part determines how you feel about the work you do and the quality and quantity of your work. The attitude you have about that work is a big part of your work value. My dad frequently said to me, "My son, it doesn't matter if you are a lawyer or garbage man, whatever you do, do your best and be proud of your work."

I think he said that because sometimes when he gave me a task I complained about it for a longer time than it would have taken me to do the task and be done with it. Sometimes when I said I didn't like the task he assigned he would say to me, "In life there will be lots of things you may not like to do, but nevertheless need to be done and you may be the only one to do them." As an owner of a physical therapy clinic, it became necessary occasionally to plunge a stopped up toilet. Not exactly a pleasant task, but a necessary one. Sometimes I was the only available person who could do it. My dad was right.

I think of my dad often. I benefitted from his wisdom and built upon it throughout my life. At some point in my life a light went on when I realized when performing a task that I didn't like, like it or not, I would do it anyway. So why not learn to like it. A wise man once said, "All of creation is God's spiritual play. We should strive to make all we do, play." A critic said, "Well, that doesn't leave time for work" and the wise man answered, "Work isn't spiritual until it is play." Why not strive to make work spiritual?

If you lived in a vacuum it might be easier to always behave in a manner that is aligned with your beliefs and values. But, no doubt, there will be times where the laws or job requirements require you to do something that may be at odds with your value system.

Every time I treated a patient I was required to write a progress note. It was a real pain, not something I wanted to do. It seemed to me that writing a note to the insurance company didn't necessarily benefit the patient. In fact, it seemed to decrease the time I had to spend with them. This put my values at odds with my behavior. This dilemma was solved by changing my belief. Writing the note could actually benefit the patient by providing an opportunity to review the patient's progress, plan for subsequent treatments, provide what the insurance company wanted and obtain reimbursement in the process — a good trade off.

As a parent, attending your child's recital is always interesting as long as you're listening to your own child. However, one has to listen to any number of other children, not always the most exciting situation, but none-the-less, sometimes that is what parents do. Think about your activities of daily living; getting up, taking a shower, getting dressed, brushing your teeth, etc. All of these behaviors are not exciting to do, but necessary activities and you are the only one who can do them.

Behaviors are what you do. They are observable by a third party and include how neatly you do your homework and how well you listen to your mom and dad or boss, how you treat your customers, clients, patients and siblings. All of these can be described as your behavior. Sometime during your life you will be conflicted between what you think is the right thing to do based upon your value system, and what your mom, dad, teachers, siblings, or people in positions of authority tell you to do. Do you compromise your integrity and other values by doing what you were told to do? Or do you do what you think is right and risk getting punished?

This is where your belief system comes to the rescue. It acts as the mediator between your values and your behavior. You might come home from school and your parents require you to do your homework before you go out to play. You value doing your homework so you will be prepared when you return to school and will have learned something and not feel foolish if you did not complete your assignment. But you believe you could go out and play first and do your homework later. So, that's what you do. But you forget to do your homework and the next day in school you sit at your desk with downcast eyes hoping not to be called upon. You feel your anxiety level increasing. Your teacher asks you a question related to the homework and you do not know the answer. An embarrassing moment for you to experience. After school you want to go out to play but you remember you have some homework. You've learned a valuable lesson and decide to do your homework first because you believe this is a better choice. So, you've changed your behavior and your belief about when you do your homework. You feel better about yourself. No more anxiety about homework left undone. No more embarrassing moments.

In times of war, which seems to be inevitable throughout the history of human beings, the soldiers on each side are more interested in their own survival than in killing someone from the other side. Given their choice they might place self-preservation ahead of fighting. Command understands this. That is why the military has created a Culture of Brothers. When you are in the service you see one another as family, as brothers and sisters. The military knows that if you see these people as brothers and sisters you're not about to leave them if they are wounded. You will help them, risking your own life in the process. This has been a very effective way to control soldiers in combat. Believing in the sanctity of human life, the appropriate behavior is not to think about killing someone, but about helping them. In war time, killing may be necessary. Seeing your fellow soldiers as brothers and hating the enemy helps you to change your belief that sometimes it is necessary to kill.

In WWII the Japanese attacked Pearl Harbor threatening our existence. We went to war to fight for our beliefs and to force them to surrender. This involved killing Japanese people, not an easy thing to do when the sanctity of life is one of your values.

In order to reduce this apparent conflict, our belief system changed to see the Japanese as our enemies. We told stories (true or not) about their behavior and made them seem less than human, thus killing them became easier. Of course, the same was done by the other side.

Our individual survival is probably built into our genetics. Without it the human species would not exist. Even our healthcare follows these principles. Most health care workers pursue this field because they value human life and the quality of human life. They believe in learning and providing the best care feasible. They behave appropriately to support their values and beliefs. Laws and reimbursement criteria have a way of changing things. The behavior of a health care worker is determined by what is reimbursable. But what is reimbursable is not always the most effective treatment. If the health care provider did what he or she thought to be the most effective service, but it was not reimbursed by insurance companies, they would go out of business. Then they would not have any patients to treat. Initially, the healthcare worker may be frustrated because they are not able to provide healthcare they believe their patients deserve and need. In time, their belief system will change. They will see that the procedure they preferred to provide really wasn't necessary. Their belief system is the intermediary between their values and behavior. They change their belief to believe the reimbursable service is actually the better service.

These concepts will come in handy for you. They will help you to understand how your values, beliefs and behaviors are part of a dynamic system. In a leadership position you will need to influence the behavior of others. Understanding that behavior is related to their values and what their belief system might be will empower you to have greater influence. You will have greater influence because you can communicate why change is necessary and how they can maintain their values in this process. Understanding how values, beliefs and behaviors function will help you to maintain balance and alignment in your life.

Examples of the above exist everywhere. Give a few examples of how you have seen this.

_____

_____

_____

_____

_____

_____

_____

BRIAN KING, Doctor of Chiropractic:

After graduating college I headed into 'adult life.' I valued the freedom to determine my own schedule. This meant doing what I wanted, when I wanted. For the next several years my behavior included kayaking the Arkansas River from Granite through part of the Royal Gorge. I took risks negotiating class V rapids and placing myself in situations that were beyond my skill level. I thought I was only responsible for myself. The same was true with my other activities. I spent as much time playing as possible. I believed, 'This was the life.'

Years went by. I found myself asking, 'Is this it? Is this all that life has to offer?' I imagined my life through the years ahead and saw that nothing much would change. I was a Human Doing, rather than a Human Being.

My wife and I started a family. We ended up having three wonderful children, each two years apart. There are many things in life that you cannot truly be prepared for and I think parenting is one of them. It's like having all your emotions magnified. I love my children more than I thought it was possible to love. I still value determining my own schedule but now it is about scheduling time to be with my children. My behavior is more cautious regarding my activities as I want to be around for my family for a long time. I believe this is the right thing to do. So this is how values, beliefs, and behaviors are active in my life.

COMMENTS: White collar stealing is a big problem for many businesses. The thieves are usually valuable employees who have "integrity" and "honesty" as two of their core values. How do they justify their dishonest behavior? Dishonest behavior would be at odds with their values. Many justify their dishonest behavior by using their belief system to come to the rescue. "I'm not really stealing. I've been underpaid for years. They owe me this." Not a very positive way to justify this behavior.

Here is a positive example. I had to travel as part of my job but I didn't want to be away from my family. My values included being a good father. This meant being present to meet their needs and being a good provider. The travel created a conflict between my belief that to be a good father I needed to be home, at least at night, and the behavior of travel as required by my work took me away from my family.

I could quit but another job might not pay as well and require travel as well. The conflict continues. Or I could change my belief so that travel became the means to maintain my value to provide for my family and an opportunity to learn new things such as "being with the family" via a phone call. Changing my belief that traveling allowed me to be a good father and provider maintained my value to be a good father and allowed me to keep my job.

∼Chapter 9∼

INTEGRITY

When I was a young boy I remember my dad saying to me, "My son, do you know what integrity means?" Of course I had no idea what he was talking about. He said, "Well, integrity means not even lying to yourself."

The word integrity comes from the Latin word "integrates" meaning integer, whole, intact. It is the keystone of your value system. It defines you as an individual. It means you say what you mean and do what you say. I've said it before but it's worth sharing again these lines from Shakespeare's play *Hamlet*. Giving advice to his son Laertes, Polonius says, "This above all: to thine own self be true. And it must follow as the night the day; thou canst not then be false to any man."

Integrity is the keystone of your values arch as seen in Figure 7. If you don't have integrity all your values are compromised. Integrity is your moral compass. It keeps you headed in the direction you believe to be the correct moral and ethical path. If honesty is one of your values and you cheat on your homework, you will intuitively know that you have fallen off the path. You have compromised your integrity. You need to get back on the path.

VALUES ARCH

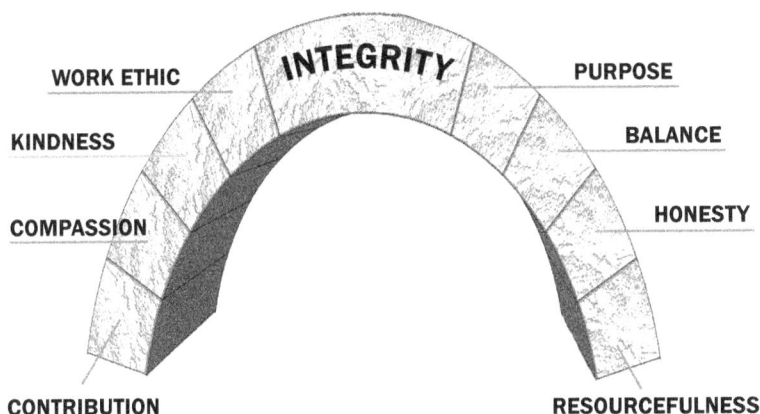

Figure 7

If having a good work ethic is one of your values and you join co-workers in goofing off when the boss leaves you've compromised your integrity. You need to get back on the path. There will be many times when compromising your integrity might seem to be the easier path to take. Sometimes telling a little white lie might make a particular situation easier for you short term but would be compromising your integrity in the process and you would know it. For example, your parents may tell you that you are forbidden to go to the mall downtown, skate-board park or some other area. A friend of your parents who is aware of this saw you at the skateboard park, or thought they did at 12:00. Your parents ask you, "Were you at the skateboard park at noon?" And you answer, "No." You're really accurate because you weren't there are noon, it was 12:15. But you know the meaning of the question and you know that what you told them was being deceitful. Your integrity was compromised because although your answer was accurate it was not truthful. You undoubtedly understand that your parents wanted to know if you were at a place where you were forbidden to be. The time is irrelevant.

You have many opportunities to decide if deviating from the path, bending your moral compass would be worth it.

Why do you think "Integrity" is the keystone in your "Values Arch?"

_____

_____

_____

_____

_____

_____

JORDAN, age 11:

I think integrity means being truthful. You need to be truthful to have friends. When you are honest you expect someone to be honest back. I want a friend to trust me with a secret and I want them to do the same. If this happens it means we have integrity in our trust with each other which makes us happy so we can have fun.

COLIN, age 12:

I wasn't allowed on the internet without permission. So, I took the matter into my own hands. I opened the internet settings on my tablet. I backspaced each letter until the "connect light button" turned bright and then went to the next letter and did the same thing. I did that until I found the password. I compromised my integrity when I did that. Even if this makes you feel smart and happy, like I am so cool it eats at you and eventually turns that good feeling into wishing I didn't do it. What I learned is it is better to be honest to yourself than be connected to the internet.

JARED, age 17:

By definition integrity means 'the quality of being honest and having strong moral principles; moral uprightness' (Oxford Dictionary). This can be lost in everyday life if you do not strive to reach for it. Integrity to me is more than the definition. It is a way some people live their lives. Everyone has a choice they can make to do right or wrong, be integral or not. But integrity has been used differently in my life. I want to become a great chef one day. In the culinary world integrity has been used to describe food. Food integrity means 'the state of being whole, entire, or undiminished or in perfect condition.' Sometimes this gets lost in gastronomical cooking, a method of breaking down food to its molecular level, then rebuilding it. Integrity in the culinary world also includes keeping truthful to what you create. Integrity is a very important part of everyday life.

MARCIA MARTINEK, Newspaper Editor:

For me, integrity means doing the right thing even when others might not even realize you've done it. It means doing the right thing even if it is not popular. Others might not like you because of what you have written, but in the end you have to like yourself. One would rather be liked than disliked, but I did not choose to be an editor because I wanted to make friends. It includes what your dad told you, "Integrity means not even lying to yourself." I must be true to myself.

Being editor of the newspaper requires me to listen and sift through what is said. Sometimes it requires reporting accurately what was said. Other times it requires a statement or a recommendation that might not be popular but is my perception of what is the right action to take. Sometimes this may not benefit the paper or me personally.

Some people can be rude or "heavy handed." This occasionally can be an emotional situation but I do my best to put emotions aside and think about what was said and not how it was said. I am dedicated to free speech. I may not agree with what was said, but I will support people's rights to say it even if I may be criticized for printing it. I believe in open government, attend many government meetings and will report as accurately as I can. Sometimes I may be wrong but I hope the paper and my writings are seen as responsible, accurate and trustworthy. In short I want to maintain my personal integrity and have the paper seen as a publication with integrity as well.

COMMENTS: I was paid a bonus by the national rehabilitation company for whom I worked for providing in-company seminars. The accounting department made a mistake and paid me twice for the same seminar. It would have been easy for me to have cashed both checks because I knew the accounting department would never catch their mistake. But it would not have been right and I knew it. So as nice as it would have been to have the extra money it was nicer to feel good about myself and return one of the checks. I am sure most folks would have done as I did and return one of the checks. But it is an example of maintaining one's integrity.

∼Chapter 10∼

MENTAL MAPS

A topo map provides a 2D representation of the area it represents by including contour lines to show you the elevation changes and other obstacles you might encounter depending on the course you've chosen. If your course takes you to a 100 foot drop-off, you might want to change course to avoid it. Mental maps do much the same thing. Mental maps are an internalized programmed way of responding to a particular event or situation. It is a map that tells us the likely outcome. It is as if you have been here before or you've heard this before and know what is going to happen. We all have unique mental maps and understanding this will help you in dealing with other individuals as well as yourself. No two people see things exactly the same.

If you look at figure 8 you'll see at the 12 o'clock position there is the word "event." This represents any event, occurrence or happening outside of yourself but it can also include your thoughts. The 3 o'clock position is the mental map. This is how you will interpret the event that you experienced. The 6 o'clock position is the behavior that is determined by your mental map and your behavior then determines the result that occurs and the cycle begins again.

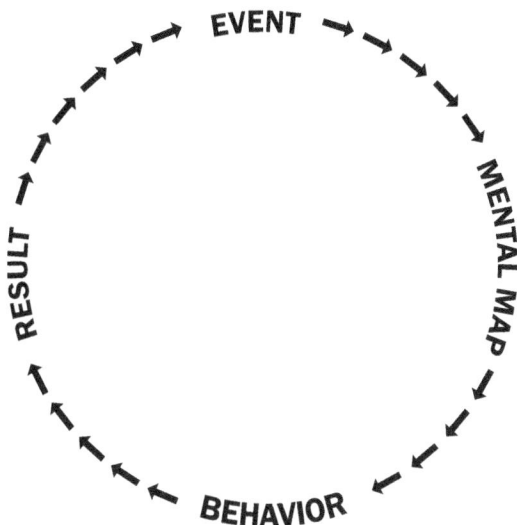

Figure 8

Our initial maps were made at a very early age, perhaps before we were eight years old. This is one reason why some young people appear to be outgoing while others are shy. Some are very adventurous and some are timid. And the quality of our maps determines the quality of our lives. Better things tend to happen to a person who has a mental map that says, "I can" or "If it is to be, it is up to me and I know I have the ability to succeed." A person whose mental map is one of failure will likely have a difficult time living a successful life.

We can choose to change our mental maps. Crisis or a very painful situation is usually what initiates a desire to change our mental map. When you get older you will come across people who are very hurried in their daily lives. Then something such as a close call with death will occur or maybe the loss of a loved one or something else that either changed or came close to changing their lives. You may hear them say, "From now on I'm going to take time to smell the roses." The lifestyle change from always needing to be someplace else to enjoying the moment was initiated by the crisis. But it can also be initiated by evaluating your mental maps and determining if they are the most effective maps for you. The value of a mental map is whether it gets you what you want. If it does, then you're doing OK. If not, then you should consider changing your mental map. Healthy individuals continually review their mental maps, reviewing their effectiveness and upgrading their quality. This is the key for exchanging a dysfunctional map that does not serve you well for an effective map that facilitates your success. Understanding this is helpful in all walks of life.

One example of how mental maps determine your behavior might be identical twins bike riding up a steep mountain. One twin is athletic and trains religiously. The other is a couch potato. They begin riding up the hill on identical bikes. Because of the effort; they both feel a burning sensation in their thighs. The athletic twin might say, "This is great; I'm getting a good work out. I'm going to work even harder." The non-athletic, couch potato twin says, "My thighs are burning, something is wrong, I better stop." This is how mental maps determine behavior and obviously the behavior described above will result in one twin becoming more fit and the other twin most likely remaining a couch potato.

Nini and I argued about living in a log cabin for years. She did not want to live in a log cabin; I thought it would be a wonderful experience. Then one day we were in Vail, Colorado looking at some of the homes and I pointed to a log cabin and I said, "That would be a wonderful log cabin to live in." Nini said, "That's not a log cabin, that's a log house." The word cabin to her engendered something that Abe Lincoln lived in when he was a young man. Obviously, it was not the same for me. It was our different mental maps regarding the same concept that caused our problem. Now we live in a wonderful log home and we're both happy.

As a physical therapist, I had occasion to treat someone who was resistant to what seemed to be a reasonable treatment for their problem. I thought it reasonable because it was a usual and customary treatment designed for their problem and I used it successfully many times. The resistant patient would tell me, "Oh, I tried those exercises before and they always make my problem worse." I told them that these exercises were designed for their problem and that I'm certain they would help them. We would initiate the exercise program and sure as the sun comes up in the east, it made their problem worse.

My ability to help these people was dramatically improved when I understood that I needed to change their mental map. In this case it was that the exercises would make their problem worse. To assist the patient in changing their mental maps I would begin an exercise program that would not stress their back but will involve the lower extremities, the ankles, knees and also the shoulders. In other words, we would begin peripherally with exercises that didn't effect their back problem. Later when they believed that these exercises did not increase their pain, we could exercise their back and core muscles. They changed their dysfunctional mental map for a more functional one. Understanding that everyone has a mental map and that these maps determine how they see things will help you serve others more effectively.

Is your mental map about short term behavior or long term results? An ineffective map focuses on techniques and tactics and fear as the primary motivation and these are all short term.

A successful map has a clear purpose and it is connected to a plan, preferably a written plan. This plan is energized by a desire to express passion and it is oriented around an internal reward system. It is focused on long term success.

How could you determine the topography (layout, content) of someone else's Mental Map? Why might this be important?

_____

_____

_____

_____

_____

_____

_____

LAUREL McHARGUE, United States Military Academy Graduate and Author:

The event for me occurred from the moment my mother handed me a shoebox full of letters my dad had written during World War II. I knew then it was time to make good on a goal I had only talked about for decades. It was time to write that first book, "Miss?" the one that would establish me as an author. I liked creative writing and storytelling. I knew I had the ability to write well (that may have been part of my mental map). I also knew I'd have to make some sacrifices to accomplish my goal. My mental map also included my belief that I would be successful and that I could do the work needed.

I had to make some behavioral changes to make this happen. I spent the next several months transposing dad's letters while learning how to actually become an author. The book was not unfolding easily. As I was writing and learning I finally realized Dad's book would not be a memoir or a WWII lesson. I wanted what he wrote in his letters to have a universal appeal and I wanted to have some fun with them. Voila! It finally hit me that I would use his letters as a diving board from which I would jump into a social commentary about the evolution of communication.

Have I finished his book? Ah ... no. But the result was that I have written two others since and have enough vignettes posted on my blog site to create a third. I have grown as a writer and support other writers in a group I began.

The outcome of all this is that I have published two books and know that I am doing what I want to do. I may not be financially wealthy from my writing but I am rich in the knowledge that I am doing with my talent what I should be doing. I believe in myself and the townspeople call me "the writer." When the time is right I will finish the book I started with Dad's letters and I know of no greater measure of success than feeling happy about what you are doing.

COMMENTS: When I was in high school I despised English, especially poetry. I thought if you want to say something why make a riddle of it? I knew I would fail so why try? I struggled through English class every year. I always flunked so I had to take it in summer school and pass or I would have to repeat my grade. Many of the other students taking summer school English said they wanted to improve their grade. I said the same thing. The difference was that they wanted to improve their grade from an 85% to 95% and I wanted to improve my grade from 50% to a passing 65%. Obviously, my mental map did not serve me well. I don't know why I didn't think to change it for a more functional map so I could play and not attend summer school.

This mental map and the accompanying behavior served to keep my grades to a level that permitted me to participate in school sports. Otherwise, I think I may have quit school if my parents would have permitted it. My grades were so poor upon high school graduation that the only school that would accept me was a community college. I attended for one semester and my mental map remained the same and after the semester I was on academic probation. I dropped out and worked for over three years. Assessment of my life revealed that I was not an overwhelming success. Something had to change and that was my mental map.

I returned to college and an English class was one of my first semester classes. Now my new map led me to the library and anthologies of selected authors whose poems I was expected to interpret. Reading what others said about a particular poem helped me to understand the poem. I liked the way the poet expressed himself. I liked the implied and hidden messages in the poems I read. I actually enjoyed English! And I did well getting "A's." In fact I was asked to join the "Knickerbocker Literary Society." Who would have guessed that? It was a result of changing my dysfunctional mental map for a more functional map.

~Chapter 11~

ATTITUDE

Attitude is not *what* you do but *how* you do what you do. It is all about your feelings. It includes how you feel about what you do and the feeling you project to others in the process. Your attitude can be described as happy, sad, positive, negative, somber, serious or light-hearted, etc. Some aspects of your attitude probably have a genetic basis. But some are learned. The bottom line is your attitude has a lot to do with the quality of your life. You can change how you respond to life's circumstances. You can change the characteristic way you behave, how you feel about things and therefore your attitude.

For example, do you see a 12 ounce glass with 6 ounces of water in it as half empty or half full? Both are accurate. If you see it as half empty you might be thought of as having a pessimistic attitude, a gloomy attitude. If you see the glass as half full you might be thought of as having an optimistic attitude, one that looks on the brighter side of things. The choice is yours to make. It seems to me that having a positive, optimistic attitude is a better choice than having a negative, pessimistic attitude. When you have a positive attitude, better things seem to come your way. You're open to new thoughts and ideas. You see opportunities where others might see threats. Negative people are difficult to be around and there seems to be no shortage of negative people. They seem to drain your energy. Negative people can be thought of as energy drainers. When you're around them you feel as though you need to recharge your emotional batteries. Positive people are easier to be with. They are energy givers. When you're around them you feel energized. People want to be around positive people.

Negative and positive people can be thought of as ducks and eagles. Negative people are like ducks, there are many more of them and they seem to flock together. They swim around together and seem to be following the leader. But if you observe their behavior closely they're really following the follower. They go wherever the leading duck takes them and hope that they will find food or not miss out on something. On the other hand, positive people are like eagles. Eagles soar higher; they see the big picture. They see the forest not just a few singular trees. They don't follow the leader, they are the leader. They see the situation more clearly. But please don't despair because inside every duck there is an eagle waiting to get out. You have a choice. You can choose to be a positive person, an eagle. See life as one of abundance. Believe that you must work to achieve your goals. Believe that, "If it is to be, it is up to me." Eagles don't wait for their ship to come in; they swim out to meet it. It has been said "opportunity knocks," meaning an appropriate time or situation for attainment of a goal or advancement is at hand. But you have to open the door. It's true that very nice things may happen to individuals who haven't lifted a finger but that doesn't happen very often. Positive people (eagles) believe in themselves and are eager to serve others.

Good things just seem to disproportionately come to people who have a positive energy-giving attitude. They are people who when assigned a task, say "try me, not why me." They know that if they can think of a goal and believe in that goal they can accomplish it. These people are can do, try me, and think out of the box, creative, energetic, positive people. These attitudes are like ripples in water. They spread. Positive people live such affirmations as, "If it is to be, it is up to me" and, "I can . . . if I think I can." The meaning is obvious, but Robert Schuler gave it additional meaning during a sermon he gave in the Crystal Cathedral. Schuler uses "I CAN" as an acronym.

The **I** in "I Can" stands for **Imagination**. Imagine yourself as you would like to be. It might mean seeing yourself as a successful student, excelling in business or athletic endeavors. It might be seeing yourself as a person who is responsive and not reactive to experiences.

The **C** is for **Commitment**. Commitment means doing whatever it takes to realize what it is that you imagine (as long as it is legal, ethical, and moral). Wayne Dyer told a story about an individual who wanted to be better at serving tennis balls. He spoke to this person about commitment and this person said, "Well, I tried." Wayne Dyer asked him, "How many times did you try?" And the answer was, "Well I tried several times and I'm still no better." Wayne Dyer told them to practice serving100 tennis balls every day. In a year that would be over 36,000 serves. At the end of the year you'll probably be better at serving tennis balls. That's commitment, doing whatever it takes to get better and never quitting.

A is for **Affirmation**. Believe you can do what you image. Napoleon Hill said, "What the mind of man can conceive and believe it can achieve." He also said that both property and riches are the offspring of thought. Think about what you imagine and believe in yourself.

Bobby Kennedy, former attorney general of the United States, whose brother John Kennedy was President, said, "Most people see things as they are and ask why. I see things as I would like them to be and ask why not."

Many individuals have achieved success doing what others said could not be done. Here's a story about the positive effects of attitude. It is the story of a fudge maker in Baltimore, Maryland. While I was in Baltimore on business I went to the mall to have lunch as an escape from the business at hand. While eating lunch I noticed there was a small fudge making business nearby. There was a kitchenette furthest away from the display case and in between the display case and the kitchenette was a marble table about 3'x4'. An employee placed the fudge on the marble table. As it started to set up it would spread out and the employee would use a paddle to push it back toward the center of the marble table. No one was watching him do this. He was not selling any fudge. People would walk by and in the meantime he continued making the fudge. He was going through the process but it didn't look like he was enjoying what he was doing.

The next day there was another employee on duty. This employee did the same thing in terms of mixing the products and putting it on the table. But then he turned his back on the table so that he was in-between the table and the display case. He would rap Elvis Presley lyrics . . . As he was rapping these lyrics the fudge was spreading. It looked as though it was going to fall off the table. Passersby would stop to watch the fudge fall off the table. Occasionally someone would say, "The fudge is going to fall off the table!" The maker of the fudge would finish the first verse, calmly turn around, take the paddle and move the fudge back toward the center. Then he would turn his back toward the fudge again and continue rapping Elvis Presley lyrics seemingly unphased. Just as he finished the second verse the fudge was moving toward the edge of the table. As though on cue he would quickly turn around just in time and move it back toward the center of the table. Before he finished there were people four and five deep around the display case watching him and also asking to buy fudge.

Both employees did the same thing making the fudge, but the second day the employee making the fudge was so entertaining that people could not help themselves. They wanted to stop and watch him rap the lyrics while making the fudge. They also purchased a fair amount of fudge. I don't know where that employee is today, but my guess is he's probably very successful at whatever it is he is doing. If you were in a position to hire one of these individuals, which one would you hire? This is a brief example of how positive affirmations and a positive attitude can affect a successful life.

The **N** in "I can" stands for **Never Give up.** Winston Churchill's biography is a worthwhile read. He faced considerable adversity on his way to becoming the Prime Minister of England during WWII. He was asked to speak at a graduation ceremony of a school he attended. It was reported that he gave the following speech, "Never… never….never….never…give up" and then sat down. Winston Churchill was persistent when most others would have quit. Energy and persistence can conquer all things.

Another important concept regarding attitude is to have an attitude of gratitude. Be thankful for every moment of your life. It's all you have, the moment. In the movie, "Dead Poets Society" starring Robin Williams, his character tries to live by the motto, "Carpe diem." Latin for seize the day. Not a bad motto but the day is too long a time period. All you really have is the moment, a dividing point between the past and the future. A very small point if it exists at all. Perhaps a better motto is "Carpe momento" meaning "Seize the moment."

People who truly live seizing the moment are positive. They think out of the box, have a try me, can-do attitude, and are energy-giving people. They are people who realize that success only comes before work in the dictionary. Not a bad idea to strive to be one of these people and surround yourself with other "carpe momento" individuals. It's all about choices.

It is said, "Attitude determines Altitude" or "How you are behaving speaks so loudly I can't hear what you are saying." What do these mean to you?

_____

_____

_____

_____

_____

_____

JOSH ADAMSON, age 25:

In life, very few things can change how you experience something more than your attitude surrounding the experience. During my five years as a United States Marine I was subjected to countless new experiences many of which I did not care to experience. Getting stationed in Okinawa, Japan was one of these. Now you may think this sounds like an excellent opportunity to experience the world, but when I received orders saying I was to be stationed there for two years, I did not have a positive outlook. My attitude directly impacted the experience I had on that island. To me, it felt like a low security penal colony with entirely too many rules to follow, and maybe it was to an extent but I felt this severely impacted my outlook. Sadly, I turned to alcohol as a coping mechanism. I realize this in hindsight mind you, but at the time I was unaware. The culture of Marines on that island revolves almost entirely around the consumption of alcohol (well, the Marine Corps in general) and I allowed myself to sink into it. I traveled the world. I got to experience Guam, Thailand, the Philippines, and mainland Japan. Despite all this my attitude remained negative and pessimistic. It's only now that I realize this. I wasted two years of my life.

This applies to any situation. In life, you will encounter many things that you simply do not want to do. Dwelling on that narrows the scope of the experience so that all you see is the negative. Going into all situations with an open mind and a positive attitude will take you far. It will not always be easy. Some situations may seem impossible but making the effort will only improve your quality of life.

Since making the decision to quit using alcohol I've had to use my attitude to cope with life's hardships. Alcohol masked how I experienced the world and now I've realized that I want to live these moments unclouded even if they are negative, sad or frustrating. Changing my attitude has allowed me to experience life realistically. Within the first year after changing my attitude I lost 40 pounds, completed the Marine Special Operations training, received a promotion and ended my active duty with the Marine Corps with an honorable discharge. My life is in my hands and my attitude has never been more positive.

LARISSA HANSEN, Restaurant Manager:

Some time ago, I worked for an airline as a flight attendant. Once I was on a flight with a very unhappy traveler. He acted as though he didn't want to be there. He could be categorized as an energy drainer. I felt like I didn't want to be there either. I realized I was letting that person affect me in a negative way. I decided not to let that happen and instead improve my attitude and be an energy giver.

Now as a restaurant manager I understand the importance of attitude even more. Being an energy giver affects those around me in a positive manner. This is true whether they are employees or customers. In the restaurant business customers will forgive an unsatisfactory meal but will not forgive unsatisfactory service. There is no second chance.

Everyone has a bad day once in a while. But my problems belong to me and no one else. I need to 'check my problems at the door.' The same could be said about our customers but I can't expect them to 'check their problems at the door.' I may not know what problems they are struggling with, I can only display an attitude that may make their time at my restaurant a pleasant one.

With a positive energy giving attitude you enjoy life more and better things seem to come along.

WENDY SLAVIN, Probation Supervisor, 5th Judicial District State of Colorado:

Your beliefs, feelings and values impact your attitude. The experiences you have over the years frame the lens through which you see the world. This lens helps you to be open minded or close minded, positive or negative or something in-between. This is true not only for the individual but for an organization as well. My staff and I continually work to cause our collective attitude to be one of open mindedness and positive in nature. We encourage mutual respect and consideration between ourselves, our clients and with those with whom we interact.

Empowering clients from different walks of life to develop and implement plans to improve their lives is incredibly rewarding. Like all jobs ours can be challenging. For example, working with clients who have addictions or mental illness isn't easy. Even though most of our clients want to do the right thing, motivating people to make long lasting positive change can be laborious. It's important to remember that changing one's attitude, behaviors or friends can be a titanic endeavor and often takes time and support and encouragement from others.

When clients are navigating frustrating or disappointing situations it is essential that they have access to a team of supportive individuals. Our collective attitude and clients improving their outlook are two of the many reasons our success rate is 78%, much higher than the state average.

FERNANDO MENDOZA, Undersheriff:

When I began my career in law enforcement I was occasionally frustrated and upset with how some things were handled. I thought about what I might do differently and what impact that might have on my staff. I believed that in my professional life and in my private life having a positive attitude changes the perspective on things. It is not always easy to remain positive but attitude goes a long way as far as leadership is concerned. I am an exam-

ple of how I want my co-workers to behave. If I have a positive attitude it will have a positive effect on my staff.

Fostering a positive attitude makes it easier to institute new policies and procedures. It makes it less stressful in a job where stress is present by the nature of what we do. I try to recognize the contribution my staff makes and let them know I appreciate what they do. I can tell the impact I have by how we treat one another.

A good attitude even helps in responding to stressful and potentially dangerous situations. My attitude and how I handle the situation will have an effect on how those involved will react. This is true even with arrestees! If I am calm and respectful with arrestees often the situation can be de-escalated. It is about understanding what the other person may be feeling. I have even had some who were arrested thank me later for arresting them. It may have prevented them from a more serious situation and gave them time to think about what they might do to improve their lives.

I feel good about what I have accomplished both in my professional and personal life. In this line of work it is easy to become negative. It is not always easy but I work to stay positive and I am proud to be part of the reason we have a positive working environment.

COMMENTS: *(Note 1)* I needed to work while attending college. I was in a work study program but it didn't pay enough for me to pay my rent so I got a job at a local food and fuel store. It paid more but still not enough. A truck driver frequented the store and told me he was making almost three times what I was making. The next day I went to the truck warehouse and applied for a job as a delivery man. This job included unloading the freight off of a trailer and placing it in the proper position on the loading dock to be loaded on an in town delivery truck. The work was cold in the winter and hot in the summer. We were required to join the Teamsters union. We all worked at the same pay rate. The work could be boring to say the least. Some of the workers would actually climb over the freight in the trailers to lie down to avoid some work. This was difficult for me to understand as it was probably over 100 degrees in the summer and freezing in the winter, not to mention cheating our employer. If attitude determines altitude these guys were below sea level.

A friend and I decided to make a game of unloading the trailers. It became a contest of who could unload a trailer first. We also made it a contest to see who would unload the delivery truck first. We were more productive than the other employees and had more fun in the process. It was a matter of attitude. It makes all the difference.

(Note 2): Richard Simmons was a popular fitness guru in the 1980s. He had his own TV program and appeared on many others. For some he was "over the top." Google his name and you will see why some might feel this way.

He came to Omaha, where I owned a physical therapy outpatient office, and appeared in the open at the University of Nebraska Medical Center campus. I was curious and went to watch the circus. The audience was filled with skeptical folks, many of whom did not like Richard Simmons.

Simmons appeared and in a few minutes he had won over the most ardent skeptic and had everyone jumping up and down following his instructions. You couldn't help but like the guy! It was his "I can do this and I care about you" attitude that won everyone over. That's the power of attitude!

~Chapter 12~

RESPONDING VERSUS REACTING

Responding and reacting are very different ways to cope and be-have with things that happen to you. Reacting is largely an emo-tional behavior. It is the flight or fight response that drives this behavior. Initially it may be satisfying but long term it does not resolve the situation.

The opposite of being reactive is being responsive. You are think-ing as well as feeling. You're always aware of your feelings but you don't let them drive you to act impulsively.

Being responsive allows you to maintain your sense of self-worth. This is extremely rewarding. Your thoughts and feelings about how you think others feel about you no longer drag you into a pit of self-doubt. You will see all sorts of new options and choices in your dealings with other people because your perspective and your sense of reasoning are not being blurred by emotions. Responsiveness can put back into your hands a good deal of control over your life. (Susan Forward, PhD, Toxic Parents)

Much of the trouble people experience is the result of being reactive and not responsive. It doesn't matter if it's first grade, eighth grade or your senior year in high school, college or working career. Most problems occur when someone says something to you that "rubs you the wrong way." Generally, this results in one of two actions: either becoming aggressive and saying something you might later regret or running away from the situation. Neither is good, although it is a good idea to take some time to think about what your response should be. Think about who said what they said, why they said it and what the appropriate response to create a win-win solution for those involved might be. Remember you are only responsible for yourself. You cannot control the behavior of others. Why would you want to live your life around those things over which you have no control? Figure 9 shows this in graphic form and is an algorythm that might make it easier to respond than to react.

Figure 9

There are three circles. The inner circle is very small and represents those things over which you have control. Those things over which you have control are very few. The only thing you really have control over is how you behave and that's difficult enough.

The next concentric circle, with a larger diameter, represents those things over which you have influence. You don't control these things but you can influence them. You can influence how others respond to you. You can influence the decisions that are made in school or work even though you may not be able to control them.

The largest diameter circle, too big to fit on this page, represents those things over which you have concern but neither control nor influence. There are many things that occur every day in your life over which you have concern but have neither control nor influence. Who is the President? What are the tax laws? What's happening in the world in terms of wars, famine, etc.? You have no control or influence over them but as an informed citizen you do have concern. The important thing is to understand this concept and apply it to your interactions with others.

You can control what you think and how you behave. Self-control is where your efforts can be most successful. Influencing others will help you get what you want — admission to the school of your choice, a good job and other things important to you. This is important because everything you want requires cooperation with others. It would be very helpful for you to understand how to influence the behavior of others.

You will always have areas of concern over which you have no control and no influence. As a responsible citizen you should be aware of events that fall into this category. But since you have neither control nor influence you should not have an emotional investment in those areas. This is easier said than done. This is why some people don't want to know about current events, it is too upsetting. Not being emotionally invested in areas of concern requires continual practice but is worth the effort. That way you can be aware of what is happening without becoming upset by what you see or hear.

Give one example of areas of Concern, Influence and Control from your own life.

_____

_____

_____

_____

_____

_____

_____

ELLIE age 10:

I got in a fight with my brother and I was so mad I hit him in the head with a metal bat (not very hard). I learned I should respond with my words and not react with anger. I learned this because I felt really bad about hurting Colin and because he pretended to be unconscious and I got in trouble with my mom and dad.

97

KEVIN KING, Doctor of Chiropractic:

As I gain more maturity in life I realize how important understanding the concept of reacting vs. responding is to one's success. I think all of us can relate to stressful confrontations and how we might want to react immediately with words or actions that will make us feel justified but that will almost certainly result in a negative outcome. As I'm driving to Denver with my kids I have encountered stressful situations on occasion. Owen, my youngest is pulling on Chloe's hair because she ate his animal crackers. My initial desire is to react by yelling at Owen, maybe pulling over the car and spanking him. But a better way is to respond to this situation by taking time to fully understand the situation. The response to this situation is to move Owen to another seat in the car so that he can no longer pull his sister's hair, and then take the animal crackers from both.

I work in the service and healthcare industry. Helping patients is my goal. Sometimes patients complaining to me about their pain can start to wear on me. My initial thought might be, "Get over it, there are so many people worse off than you!" But responding instead of reacting helps me to realize that this person only knows their own experiences and needs to be heard. They need someone who can help them through their tough time by being compassionate and responding in an empathetic way. This helps me to be more effective in the services I provide.

COMMENTS: I was a hot reactor when I was young. I was always ready to react to the question: "What are you looking at?" I was always facilitated to initiate the first part of the "fight or flight" concept. Almost always this mode of behaving (reacting) resulted in a less than desirable outcome. It was only when I learned to take time to think about what response would yield a desirable outcome to whatever situation arose that things became easier for me. Except for those emergency situations where a quick reaction is necessary and desirable, having been on both sides of this equation leads me to believe that responding is much better than reacting.

∼Chapter 13∼

VALUING DIVERSITY

Valuing diversity has become a mantra in our society. Educational institutions, businesses and even individuals profess to value diversity. But what does this mean? Diversity means to recognize differences in people. To value differences means to recognize differences as being useful, good, worthy of consideration and thought.

While one may profess to value diversity, usually it is that diversity is tolerated and not valued. Tolerate means one believes their position to be intellectually or morally superior. This is true even when the diversity is of thoughts or ideas. When ideas are not valued but merely tolerated divisiveness often occurs. It becomes us and them. Someone has to be the winner and someone else has to be the loser. One party is right and the other wrong. When the facts do not support one party's opinion the facts are simply overlooked. In the courtroom when the evidence cannot be refuted the attorney will attack the witness. When a message is not appreciated it is the messenger that is attacked. Not a very mature approach. Even worse, the opposing party may be vilified.

Companies that do not value diversity of ideas become stagnant, are not creative, do the same things over and over. People and communities can suffer from this same thing. Diversity of ideas can be beneficial. It is by valuing diverse ideas that a solution to a problem that would otherwise remain unsolved can occur. It is not easy, but it is rewarding to learn to value diversity of ideas. Aristotle said, "I count him braver who overcomes his own desires than he who conquers his enemies. For the hardest victory is the victory over self."

Valuing diversity is not an easy value to achieve; it takes a lot of work. It means admitting you might be wrong. It means recognizing the value of others even though they are different from you, even though you may feel uncomfortable with someone else's religion, race, ethnicity, or ideas. But the effort is worth the work. It is through a diversity of ideas that the best solution to a problem is found. It can be a solution that is better than any of the parties involved might come up with by themselves.

BUD ELLIOTT, Businessman, Former Mayor and County Commissioner Candidate:

I have been trying to practice valuing diversity before I applied that term to the process. I have always thought it necessary to involve others in the decision making process. If we only do what we have always done the result will be the same. I know I don't have all the answers; sometimes I don't even have all the questions. By involving others I occasionally learn things about which I was unaware.

Often we become so entrenched in a position it is hard to be objective and understand other points of view. But it is necessary to work together to consider the needs of all. I try to listen to others, respecting facts and opinions that I may not always agree with but it is by this process that change is possible. It takes time and willingness to change and the understanding that the best decisions are made by input from numerous resources.

Some of the issues I faced as Mayor, and will face as a County Commissioner, are complex. Not everyone is enthusiastic about decisions that are made. I think that by listening to the input of others and valuing what they say, I can prepare our citizens for change and explain why the decision made may be the best action to take. I know that in an elected position I represent all our citizens. I am not perfect but by valuing diversity I will be able to earn their trust which will help us all.

It is important to make myself available to another's views and opinions when I can predict they may be very different from my own. It helps me to know that I have considered different values related to an issue that may be very controversial. Controversial issues can become much less so if those affected know that their values have been considered and I may find my way to a very different view myself from what I initially considered. Non-controversial issues can become very polarizing if those you are pledged to serve feel their views are not important enough to be heard.

COMMENTS: When diversity is the topic most people think of valuing diversity in religion, race and gender. These are important but even more important is diversity in ideas. But valuing diversity in ideas may be the toughest of all. It means listening to those who may think differently than you do. This is not always easy. It means you have to listen to different ideas and value those ideas. It doesn't mean you give up your own ideas but that you realize your idea might not be the best idea and that there are alternatives.

∾Chapter 14∾

QUESTION AND ANALYZE

We live in a society where deceit seems to be acceptable. Did you ever buy something only to find out after you have purchased it that batteries were not included? Or have you purchased an electronic device such as a computer or notepad only to discover that the charging unit was not included. And later when you purchase an automobile you'll find that there's a considerable handling and delivering fee they neglected to tell you about. Or when closing on a house you are charged a "loan origination fee" which is a substantial amount of money. All of these things will leave you smacking your palm to your forehead and wondering why you weren't made aware of these things before your purchase. Learning about some of these things is your responsibility as an informed consumer. But some things are nearly impossible to know before you experience them. So it is almost always a good idea to question and scrutinize everything.

Questioning means you are giving serious consideration to what is said or written. A questioning attitude means you value what others say and you would like more information regarding how they formed a particular opinion. That isn't always easy because people are firm in their beliefs and if you question them they don't always accept this graciously. So you have to be careful how you ask a question. Instead of saying, "I don't believe that," you might say, "I am sorry but I don't understand. Please help me to understand. Can you explain that to me?"

My dad said, "Believe none of what you hear and half of what you see." What personal, professional, financial and spiritual goals you develop will require thought and some research. But who and what do you believe? The internet is filled with opinions that are presented as facts, but are they valid facts? The news is presented as factual but is it opinion based upon what will improve their ratings? It seems that fact checking is not usually of concern to the news editors. Fact checking is left up to you. So, be careful about how you develop your own opinions. Make sure you base your opinions on the facts as well as you can determine what the facts might be.

We all have biases, positions or preferences regarding how we feel about the things we do, how we interpret what we see, and even how we think. Being biased is a human trait. We all have biases and can't avoid it at least not entirely. There is nothing wrong with having biases as long as you realize they exist and as long as you don't let biases interfere with the facts. There are those who would not let the facts modify their opinion or belief. The tendency is to interpret even objective information in a way that reinforces biases. It is interesting to note the more education a person has, the better they are at defending their biases. You might think this doesn't seem right. Many think the more one "knows to be true" the more accurate their arguments. However, facts change as new information is acquired or a different way of looking at existing facts becomes popular. If you think knowledge is facts you may spend valuable time defending your position and not enough time learning the new facts that might cause you to change your opinion. If you do this, you may become a dinosaur and you know what happened to them.

This is where questioning is important. To question means to think about what you hear and read and not just accept it because the person who said it is someone you respect. You will hear many things in your lifetime that are hard to believe. You could accept what is said as fact, especially if the overwhelming majority of your peers accept them. You might think you do not have the experience, education or intellect to disagree with what you see or hear but your concerns may be justified. Get the facts and think about them. Form your opinion based upon those facts, remembering that facts can and do change. At one time, it was a fact that the sun revolved around the earth. It was fact that the earth was flat. It was fact that it would be physically impossible to break the sound barrier and that the smallest subatomic particle was the electron.

It is prudent to be questioning of everything you see, hear, read and even experience. Require proof for what is being presented. With all of the information available on the internet and no fact checkers determining the veracity of what is presented, we are living in an era where misinformation abounds. Questioning and analyzing are very important attributes. This may sound cynical but no matter who says something or how well intended they are, you need to do your homework.

We recently visited Rocky Mountain National Park. We were taking a hiker shuttle to the trailhead to go for a hike. The driver of the shuttle was a very nice man who was trying to make the trip enjoyable and informative for everyone on board. He spoke about the animal life, the plant life and some of the other things we were looking at as we made our journey toward the trailhead. One of the things he mentioned was that the pine beetle had decimated a particular camping area. That area needed to be clear cut as a result. He also mentioned that the trees the beetle affect are the lodge pole pines that were used by the Indians for their teepee poles because they are tall and skinny. He said, "That's the nature of lodge pole pines; they grow tall and skinny." Now it is true that the Indians used those for their teepees but that's not always the nature of the lodge pole pines. They only grow tall and skinny when they are in what is called a hounds-hair forest. That is where they grow very close together so they must grow tall and skinny to get light. So they don't get very large in diameter. But if a lodge pole pine is in the middle of a meadow it gets to be a very full tree. This gives an example of how misinformation is present everywhere and how questioning and analyzing can be beneficial.

Our form of government is called a republic. A republic means we elect others to represent us in a manner that provides for the common good. We elect our representatives based on what they say and do. But with the stakes so high and the desire to get elected so strong, can you truly believe what they say? Sound bites and mottos may sound good but what do they actually mean? What is the candidate proposing and could what they are proposing actually work? Thinking critically takes a lot of work but it is what must be done if you hope to make an intelligent voting decision.

When I was in 7th grade in Catholic school, I remember the nuns saying that our form of government requires an educated electorate. At the time, I remember thinking how much education do you need to pull a lever in a voting booth? Now I know what they meant. Questioning and analyzing is important to participating in our form of government. It is also useful in your education and the work you choose to do.

How can Questioning and Analyzing help you?

_____

_____

_____

_____

_____

_____

_____

BRENNAN, age 8:

My friend tells stories to impress me and other friends. He makes up stories about video games and things his dad has done. It's hard to tell when he is telling the truth and when he is lying. I had to question and analyze what he said. I kinda think about if the things he said are even possible. I ask some questions and see if what he is saying seems reasonable.

PEGGY FORNEY, Author:

I won't say that questioning and analyzing are more important than the other concepts mentioned in this book but it is the beginning of making choices or decisions that may affect life. I try to question and analyze just about everything I hear or read. What is the basis of what was said? Is it factual or opinion? If it was factual are the "facts" valid? It is by questioning that new "facts" may be discovered. This is not always easy. Sometimes questioning a speaker regarding the validity of what was said is interpreted by the speaker or others as saying that you don't believe what was said. This may not be so. All I was doing was asking for additional information for me to process what was said. This is not always met with enthusiasm. I would rather be liked than disliked but maintaining my integrity is more important than being liked.

I said that questioning and analyzing is the way to discover new "facts." One example occurred when I moved to the mountains. I was overweight but noticed my weight and body chemistry improved. I read some of the "facts" about living at altitude and they didn't match up with my personal experience. I analyzed what I read and discovered some interesting information that led me to write a book, "Healthiest Places to Live," that challenges some "facts" using objective information. Questioning and analyzing is very necessary to maximize a life of opportunity and fulfillment.

COMMENTS: Question and analyze is another way of saying be skeptical and engage in critical thinking. It doesn't matter what terms you use it is the process that is important. Today the challenge for young people, and really for all of us, is not getting information (just Google it) but knowing what information is meaningful. That's why analyzing what you've read or heard is so important. You do not want to make decisions or formulate opinions based upon invalid information. You need to analyze almost everything to the extent you aren't suffering from "analysis paralysis."

∼ Chapter 15 ∼

COMPETENCY

You may have heard people say, "They didn't know what they were doing." Usually, they are referring to the inability of someone to complete a task in an acceptable manner. This may be due to a mental or physical deficiency, a lack of education, a lack of training, or an "I don't care attitude." Regardless of the reason, what they're talking about is a lack of competency. But competency may not be quite as simple as it sounds because there are four levels of competency.

Unconscious Competence
Conscious Competence
Conscious Incompetence
Unconscious Incompetence

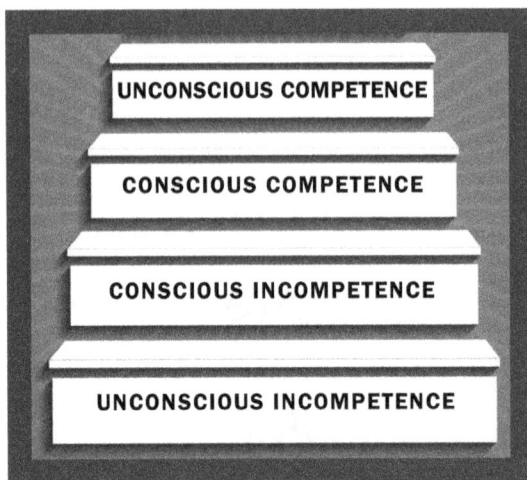

Figure 10

The levels of competence can be thought of as four stairs to climb as you can see in figure 10. Whenever something new is attempted the first step must be taken. That step is the lowest level of competence, **unconscious incompetence**. This means that the person cannot perform a task or an activity to the level expected because they're unaware of what is required. I remember being at Pismo Beach, California hunting for clams with friends who thought this would be a fun thing to do. I was digging up clams as fast as I could. There is a measuring device on the pitch fork used to dig clams indicating that most of the clams I was digging up were too small to keep. I was throwing them over my shoulder and continuing to dig for a clam that would be large enough to keep. I didn't know that you're supposed to put clams that are too small back into the sand, under the water so they could grow and not float around and become a sea gull snack. I was at a level of unconscious incompetence. I didn't know that I didn't know what I was doing.

While hiking in a forest I saw two women wearing flip flops climbing a snow bank thinking it would be fun to slide down. What they didn't know was that although they might have fun sliding down the snowfield a boulder at the end of the snow field could end their slide abruptly. That could lead to a very undesirable outcome. They were unaware of the dangers in what they were doing. They were at the level of unconscious incompetence.

The next higher level or step of competence is **conscious incompetence.** This means, you don't know what you're doing but at least you know that you don't know what you're doing. You might be learning to shoot a bow and arrow and be unaware of what side of the bow to place the arrow. Knowing that you don't know this at least puts you at the level of conscious incompetence. However, you might also be at the level of unconscious incompetence if you didn't know that when you draw back on the bow string and release it that if you're not looking the right way the bow string could just about take off your nose. This would result in a fast learning experience.

The next level or step of competence is **conscious competence**. At this level you are competent but only when you think about it. When you were learning to drive, you have to see the stop sign and think about taking your right foot off the accelerator and putting it on the brake pad. You have to be consciously aware of the inherent dangers in driving. As long as you do these things you're competent. But one of the problems that new drivers have is that they are competent only if they are paying focused attention. As you gain more skill you will achieve a higher level of competence, which is the final step, **unconscious competence.**

At the level of unconscious competence you drive the car, stop at the stop sign or stop at a traffic light if it is red. You have to do this enough times to have unconscious memory of how to perform appropriately. You are competent without thinking about it.

We all experience various levels of competency depending upon what it is that we are doing. Things that we are trained for, educated for, things that we have repetitive experience in doing may bring us to the level of unconscious competence. However, if you are learning new skills throughout your life, you will find yourself at various levels beginning with unconscious incompetence proceeding up to and including unconscious competence.

It's interesting to note some people use these various levels of competence to help themselves in any particular situation. For example, Peyton Manning, who recently played quarterback for the Denver Broncos, is at the level of unconscious competence in his quarterbacking. He looks at the defense, sees how they are lined up and understands from his previous experience and study what they are likely to do. He will adjust his offense, take the snap from the center, step back and throw a pass, expecting what his offensive team will do and what the defense will do based upon how they were lined up. What the defense does is rely on his level of unconscious competence and show him a defense that would cause him to throw a pass in a certain area of the field. At the last second the defensive team changes alignment hoping to foil the play. The outcome of the play will depend upon who guessed right.

Later in your life if you are a supervisor of employees or you have your own business it is helpful to observe others and see in which stage of competence they are performing so that you can help them move toward the highest level of competence, unconscious competence.

How does understanding the Levels of Competency help you?

_____

_____

_____

_____

_____

_____

_____

MIKE BORDOGNA, County Commissioner:

As a young person self-doubt was a great motivating factor for me. I wanted to be prepared in whatever I did. When I ran for County Commissioner I knew there were some people who didn't care for me. This caused me to try even harder.

When I became a County Commissioner I quickly learned there were many things I didn't know and came to realize that there were some things I didn't know I didn't know. I spoke with past County Commissioners, residents, visited with County Commissioners in other counties, read as much as I could and attended many county meetings in order to get a feeling about how the various community challenges were weighed by the greater community.

In some areas I function at the level of unconscious compe-
tence but there are too many areas I am responsible for it is not
possible to function at that level all the time. I tried sometimes
working longer and harder in order to address more issues but at
the expense of my health and happiness. County Commissioners
are responsible for making policy, creating budgets, managing the
fire and sheriff, public health, public transportation, emergency
management, planning for growth, water rights and many other
areas of concern. It is just not possible to function at the level of
unconscious competence in all areas.

Being a County Commissioner is a balance between what
is the right thing to do and what some citizens want to have
happen, between what is feasible and what is imagined. I have
learned to trust my own instincts modified by the experience
of others whom I trust because of their areas of expertise and
their judgement.

COMMENTS: We are all in various levels of competence depending upon what we are doing and how many times we have done it. I
worked in the mail room for I.B.M. in New York City. One of my jobs
was to "coop" the mail which meant putting it in the correct place in
one of about 200 vertical bins which were above a table where the
mail was placed. The other mail boys were "cooping" the mail faster
than I could read the address. I felt so inadequate. I was at the level
of conscious incompetence. I thought I'd never be able to do this. It
wasn't long before I was performing at a rate equal to the others.

The purpose of defining your level of competence is to recognize at what level you are performing and know what you need to
do to improve.

∼ Chapter 16 ∼

DEVELOP A SUCCESSFUL LIFESTYLE

Did you ever wonder why some people succeed while success seems to elude others? Why do some who are born and raised in a disadvantaged and dysfunctional environment achieve a high level of success while others seem to exhibit dysfunctional behaviors? Let me be clear about what I mean by success. Success is a favorable outcome any way you define it. However you define success, it is important to include all aspects of your life: professional, personal, financial and spiritual.

You may have heard it said, "Some succeed because they are destined to. Most succeed because they are determined to." If you rely on destiny, you'll only have luck on your side. That would be easy since you only have to wait around to win the lottery, find a giant gold nugget or get discovered by some movie producer or some other unexpected and unearned stroke of good fortune. Who would not appreciate a stroke of luck? Someone once said, "I really believe in luck. How else would one explain the success of those you don't like?" But luck is capricious. I would prefer something a bit more certain.

If you are determined to succeed there are some simple steps that you can follow to increase your chance of being successful. The first step is to believe in yourself. Believe that you have the ability to succeed. You only need the desire associated with a plan to achieve your desires. Henry Ford said, "Whether you think you can or think you can't, you're right." Believe in yourself and live a successful lifestyle. Ben Franklin said, "Early to bed and early to rise makes a man healthy, wealthy and wise." Getting up early has many benefits. Sunrise is often the most beautiful time of the day. Whatever you do, it will be easier earlier in the day, whether it's going for a walk or run, grocery shopping, reading or just planning your day. There are fewer people to slow you down earlier in the day. Your chances of getting a job are better if you are the first to apply and be interviewed. Be aware that by being the first (or one of the first) you may be the benchmark to which all others are compared. So be at your best. But some might say, "I like to stay up late and I like sleeping in." So be it, it's their choice. Like it or not our society favors those who follow Ben Franklin's advice.

Early to bed means you won't be spending much time watching entertaining but mindless TV programs, or playing video games that may not have a positive effect on your future. By going to bed early you'll also be more rested than the average American who according to statistics is about two hours sleep deprived every night. These two things, early to bed and early to rise will give you a head start with your competition, whether it is in school, at the work place or any other aspect of your life. At some time in your educational career you will be assigned a paper to write. Usually it's assigned the first weeks of class for completion the last few weeks of the semester. Most students will wait until the last minute to complete and hand in the assignment. Their paper is completed in haste and the instructor is swamped with papers to grade in a short period of time. How do you think you would feel if you were the instructor? You would have to read the papers quickly, probably be a bit more reluctant to give superior grades. On the other hand, if the assignment given in the first week of the semester was handed in early, your instructor will be pleased to get the paper and read it more leisurely. You are more likely to get a higher grade than others who are preparing their papers while you are studying for final exams.

In all you do, think about serving others because it is the right thing to do. It is true that the better you meet the needs of others the better you will do as a consequence. Think of the places where you do repeat business. It might be a restaurant, retail or service business, vacation spot or website. Think about the individuals you interact with in these businesses. Your returning to these businesses is a result of how well they meet your needs. Their desire to "wow" you with what they do is part of a successful lifestyle.

What do you do to live a Successful Lifestyle?

_____

_____

_____

_____

_____

_____

MIKE McHARGUE, Graduate of the U. S. Military Academy, Lt. Col. (retired), Director, Office of Emergency Management:

Each person's definition of success is going to be different. For some soul searching or internal dialog is necessary to determine what success is going to look like for you. Part of developing a successful lifestyle is deciding what you are passionate about. If you are passionate about your occupation it will not feel like work. If you are not passionate about it, then it becomes just a job. What else are you passionate about aside from your occupation? What logical set of things leads to success in that specific discipline or activity?

I loved being in the military. I especially loved working with the cadets at the Academy and new soldiers who would accept challenges without hesitation or concern over how painful the experience might be. These individuals had unbridled enthusiasm, which is an important trait for personal growth and achievement.

Now, I am fortunate in my position as Emergency Manager for the county because I believe in what I am doing. For me, being successful is not just about me, it's the whole community. Being prepared as a community requires the involvement and cooperation of many. My success is measured by how well this cooperative effort benefits everyone. Over the years I've coordinated community meetings to prepare and plan for potential county disasters such as fires, or floods or other hazards. One aspect of my job is to ensure that all of our response agencies have plans to address these potentially devastating events, and without scheduling training exercises to evaluate progress and identify shortfalls, we wouldn't be as prepared as we are now to deal with a county-wide crisis. With each exercise we complete – and these exercises take months of coordination with all the different agencies – confidence in our ability to work together in a crisis grows. I think that's a measure of success.

The U. S. Marines are being trained to have "an action bias," meaning they respond proactively to situations and translate thought into action. I think this is a good policy and I've always tried to be action oriented. Having a good idea isn't really helpful if you can't put it into action. One thing you'll have to do when focusing on what you're passionate about is to minimize, then often eliminate, things that would interfere with the goals you've set.

I set goals for my life beyond my job as well. For me to be successful, I try to prioritize my day, carving out time for what I need and want to accomplish. This includes time for exercise and self-development which often involves reading and time for family. Near the end of each year, I establish my personal goals for the upcoming year, and with my wife, we establish some family goals such as when we'll take vacation time. If we don't put it on the calendar, it won't happen.

With everything I do I try to have it be a building block to a larger goal. I'm realistic about my abilities, but I know that if I don't push against my internal boundaries, I may become increasingly more risk adverse and that would limit what I do. I like to pick goals that are outside my comfort zone and work toward them anyway, because those goals help me grow as a person, which I think is an important aspect of living a successful lifestyle. If you aren't intentional about what you are doing each day, you can't build the foundation to be successful. If I am living out my plans for the goals I've set, I'm living a successful lifestyle.

COMMENTS: There are things you have to do if you don't want to be a social outcast. You have to take care of your personal grooming needs, comb your hair, brush your teeth, dress yourself, shower occasionally so you don't stink. So why not do these things in a manner that might help you get what you want? Like it or not a red Mohawk haircut might get you attention but not be the best haircut for doing well in an interview to obtain a job or getting into a school.

You have the same time that everyone else has, 24 hours in a day, 7 days in a week, etc. Why not use this time wisely. Instead of playing video games or spending time on social media or taking selfies, read a book, help someone, and learn something that will help you. I know you have to have fun but you could make these things fun. You have to decide what you would like your life to be like. Developing a successful lifestyle will make it easier for you to succeed in whatever you want to do in whatever phase of life you are in.

∼Chapter 17∼

COMMUNICATION

Communication is the process of getting what one person is thinking to be understood by another person or group of people. It involves not just speaking but hearing, seeing, touching and other senses as well. Communication is a science but also an art. That is why some are better communicators than others.

Perhaps the most important skill in communicating effectively is listening. Listening is different from hearing. Hearing is a passive physiological phenomenon. It is measurable and may be augmented by hearing aids or other procedures to increase a person's ability to hear sounds.

Listening requires active participation. It involves listening to what another is saying, interpreting it and determining how you might respond. It means truly wanting to understand what another is saying and how they feel about what they are saying.

How many times have you been talking to someone and almost before you stop speaking they begin to tell you what they were thinking? They weren't listening to you but waiting for an opportunity to tell you what was on their mind. Would it not be better to "Seek first to understand then to be understood," as Stephen Covey so eloquently said?

Listening has many benefits. People tend to like those who seem interested in what they are saying. When you listen you may learn something that can be of benefit to you and others as well. You can become a better problem solver because you do not dominate the conversation, you give others the opportunity to talk, and are willing to listen to other ideas. You learn to be patient. You learn to be accepting and not just tolerant (which implies you believe your viewpoint to be of superior value) of the differences between yourself and others.

Effective communication also involves paying attention to the emotion behind what the person is saying. Do they appear to be upset, nervous, relaxed, informative, persuasive, aggressive, or display some other emotion? Are they speaking in a loud voice or a soft voice? There is usually some emotion behind what someone is saying. Clues such as posture, gestures, facial expressions, eye movement and other physical movements and attributes all mean something. Often the unspoken part of communication is actually more important than the spoken word. There is a saying that goes something like this, "What you are doing speaks so loudly, I can't hear what you are saying." This is called body language and is a very important part of interpreting what was said. There are many ways to say "Good morning." One of the reasons e-mail or social media is not as effective as person to person conversation is that the emotion is missing. Someone may write, "My last visit with you was fun." Does this mean they don't intend to visit with you again or are they referring to their most recent visit? Remember that even though you assess what was said based upon what you believe you heard and saw, your assessment still involves some assumptions and it is almost never good to assume. It is said that to assume makes an "<u>ass</u>" out of "<u>u</u>" and "<u>me</u>." Always ask for verification. You might say something like, "This is what I understand you to have said, am I correct?" Or, "This is what I thought you said, did I understand you accurately?"

Determine how you will respond. What will you say? How will you say what you want to say? What will be your demeanor when you are speaking? In any situation where there is a difference of opinion, the person who speaks most clearly, slowly, factually in a non-emotional manner usually prevails.

Speaking or writing is the usual way one person communicates to another person. To do this requires using words. Choosing the correct words is critical to effective communication. Just about all parents of my generation mentioned more than once to their children, "Say what you mean and mean what you say."

"Awesome," a much overused word, does not describe very much. What does it mean? It is not a very good answer to "how was the movie?" Choose your words to accurately convey what you are thinking.

In all my life I have not met anyone named "Dude." People like to hear their name. For one thing it means you actually know who they are. For another it is a sign of respect.

Have you heard people, even some in very public positions say, "He walks his walk and talks his talk?" What does that mean? It means he doesn't do anything. His talk is expressing what his values are. His walk is his behavior demonstrating adherence to those values. To demonstrate that he actually adheres to his values would require him to "Walk his talk."

How about "kick-starting" something such as an education or career? This actually refers to a method of starting an internal combustion engine. Electric starters are now the standard. When people talk about kick starting something, they would be more accurate to talk about "jump starting" it. Jump start usually refers to getting the edge on the competition. In track, the starter gives the commands, "Runners take your mark, set" and then the gun goes off starting the race. Before the starting blocks were attached to electronic timing devices runners could try to time their start by listening to the cadence of the starter. Getting a jump start meant that the runner timed the start so that they began a fraction of a second before the other runners and was not guilty of a false start. So, if someone is referring to having an advantage over the competition (maybe a differential advantage) they might say they have a jump start on the competition. So choose your words carefully so they are easily understood by others. Always strive to be kind but make sure your communication style is direct, to the point and clear. That way you have a better chance of being understood.

Public speaking usually refers to delivering a planned message to a group of people. The group may be a few people or many. The principles are the same. Be organized, honest, sincere, and energetic and speak to each person, not to the group. Teachers do this every day. In business, public speaking skills are used to communicate business decisions to employees. It can take place in a public forum where local officials are being asked to approve certain requests. Public speaking may also be extemporaneous where the message was not planned but a response to what was said. Regardless of the circumstances for the presentation, public speaking skills are a very important part of your communication skills.

The reward for a job well done might be considerable but there are risks associated with public speaking. You could make a mistake or forget what you wanted to say. I have presented many seminars and occasionally have forgotten where I was and had to ask the audience for help. It was a good test to see if they were paying attention and if I remembered the fifth guideline for life, "lighten up."

However you do it learning to speak effectively to a group is very important. Take a public speaking course in school. Join Toastmasters organization which is a fine organization to develop your public speaking skills. It really doesn't matter where or how you develop your skills. What matters is that you do it. As in anything, the more you do the better you will get.

Writing is a skill that seems to be going by the wayside. Young people seem to prefer texting and using social media to communicate. But it is a one way communication vehicle sent loaded with abbr. and bullet points. Complete sentences are becoming a thing of the past. How can you develop a vision story (see Chapter 22) without the complete sentences necessary to communicate thoughts?

Providing vacation coverage as a physical therapist for Doctors of Physical Therapy I was astounded to read their patient notes. Rarely was there a complete sentence. After reading several pages of an initial evaluation, I was left wondering what the findings were that related to the patient's function and what the D.P.T. intended to do for the patient.

I presented a seminar where the audience consisted of well-educated professional people in the healthcare industry. I asked them to begin their Vision Story and was met with a blank look by many in the audience. I thought I said something that was not understandable. I asked what the problem was and was told they were not used to writing complete sentences.

Writing is an important skill to develop along with public speaking. No matter what path you choose to follow some writing will be necessary. Reports, instructions, summaries and other forms of written communication will be necessary. Even in the personal component of your life written communication will be important. Graduation announcements, wedding invitations, birth announcements, birthday greetings and wishes, get well messages are just a few of the times when a well written note will be important. These skills will set you apart as an individual who can make their thoughts understood by others. Since everything you want will include others these are good skills to have. No matter what you do to earn a living you will be better off if you can speak and write well. So, develop these skills. Take courses in speaking and writing. Look for opportunities to use these skills in your education and your work.

CLAY STEWART, Air Force Colonel (retired), United States Air Force Academy graduate, former SAC commander:

Communication is not an easy process. I think it consists of two steps. The first is to get what is in my mind into the mind of another. That requires me to try to understand exactly what another person means to communicate, what is inside their head. If I am successful it is because I can process information, thought, or feeling so that it is satisfactorily received or understood. The second step is for me to look at the big picture. What is the objective reality to the extent of my ability to understand it. So it stands to reason that most of my communication time is invested in listening. What is the other person seeing that I am not? What is the reality of the situation? What concerns were expressed? Are they real or perceived?

I need to recognize all their concerns and understand their position with them. It is by understanding them that I can reply appropriately. 'Seek First to Understand, Then to Be Understood,' Stephen Covey's fifth habit in his book, "The 7 Habits of Highly Effective People." Communicating can be difficult because of poor transmission lines: speaking unclearly, noise interfering with hearing, distracted listeners. Even with perfect transmission lines, communicating is still extremely difficult. People have a difficult time understanding a reality that is often complex and obscure, and they have an even greater difficulty sharing that limited, somewhat foggy understanding with each other. Only when they can share that understanding are they communicating.

The difficulty of understanding and then sharing that understanding is illustrated by two metaphors: the story of blind men touching an elephant, and Plato's allegory of seeing unclearly in a cave.

The Blind Men and the Elephant is a parable about a group of blind men who touch an elephant to learn what it is like. Each one feels a different part, but only one part, such as the leg, tail, trunk, tusk, etc. They then compare notes and learn that they are in complete disagreement about what they think they are feeling.

The blind man who feels a leg says the elephant is like a pillar; the one who feels the tail says the elephant is like a rope; the one who feels the trunk says the elephant is like a tree branch; the one who feels the ear says the elephant is like a hand fan; the one who feels the belly says the elephant is like a wall; and the one who feels the tusk says the elephant is like a solid pipe. The men cannot agree with one another and come to blows over the question of what they are feeling and what an elephant is like.

They stop talking, start listening and collaborate to "see" the full elephant. When a sighted man walks by and sees the entire elephant all at once, he explains to them what they are feeling and how all of their perspectives add up to be an elephant. In addition, the blind men also learn they are all blind.

While one's individual understanding can be true, such understanding is inherently limited by its failure to account for other truths, other people's understanding and perspective, or a totality of truth, establishing the need for communication, respect for different perspectives, and sharing different understandings.

This parable resolves the conflict, and is used to illustrate the principle of living in harmony with people who see things differently. People can be misled by the aspects they do understand, leading them to deny the aspects they don't understand. The parable teaches the importance of considering all viewpoints, sharing those different viewpoint, and thereby obtaining a full picture of reality.

Plato's "Allegory of the Cave" has a group of prisoners who have lived chained to the wall of a cave most of their lives, facing a blank wall. The prisoners watch shadows projected on the wall from things passing in front of a fire behind them, and they begin to give names to these shadows. The shadows are as close as the prisoners get to viewing reality.

Although the shadows constitute reality for the prisoners, because they have never seen anything else they do not realize that what they see are shadows, much less that these shadows are the result of real living things outside the cave.

Plato implies that if the people were freed from the cave, which he suggests would be highly desirable, and came to understand that the shadows on the wall actually were not reality, then the prisoners could understand the true form of reality rather than the mere shadows they have been seeing all of their lives.

Look at a puzzle, have an idea that relates, a theory as a collection of ideas to answer the puzzle, recognizing you only see part of the answer and only obscurely, so you must share your possible answer (hypotheses) with other observers and try to integrate all of your understandings into seeing the actual jewel, the elephant, the actual actors and not just shadows on the wall.

I try to remember these things as I communicate with others. It is not easy and I realize no one, including myself, is so good at communicating that we could not improve.

COMMENTS: There was a time when I would rather pick up a rattle snake, wrestle an alligator or eat a slug than give a speech. But I knew public speaking would help my career. I took a speech class in college. I hated it but I learned how to do it anyway. I once gave a speech where I went through my introduction twice not even realizing I went through it once! My knees would shake and my voice quiver. Nevertheless I persevered and the more speeches I gave the better I got until public speaking became easy and fun. It can work that way for you as well.

Sometimes communication doesn't involve what was said but what was implied. I was a mail boy at I.B.M. Part of my duties was delivering the *Wall Street Journal* to the top executives. I don't remember the accurate number but it was around 15. I would write the name of the executive on the paper and deliver it to their office. Whoever delivered the *Journals* didn't always deliver the proper number of papers. Sometimes we were one paper short. I would short one executive one time and another when we were short again. One of the executives who thought he was Mr. Big Deal complained when I shorted him. I explained why this was happening and that I didn't have the authority to talk to the paper distributer only to let my supervisor know about the occasional shortage. He told me that was my problem and that he didn't care about anyone else, he needed the paper. I wanted to get him off my back so I did the following which achieved my goal but not in the most mature manner. I went to the office of Tom Watson, Jr. (who was the Chairman of the Board and CEO of I.B.M.) and crossed out Watson's name and wrote in the name of the disgruntled executive. The implied message to Mr. Big Deal was someone thought he should have the paper and not the chairman of the board. If inquiry was made it might not be so good for Mr. Big Deal. I will say that executive didn't complain the next time he was shorted.

∾Chapter 18∾

HOW TO GET WHAT YOU WANT
By getting others what they want

Especially when you were young you probably heard people say, "Don't be selfish." Those saying it were probably trying to get you to share something with someone else. You may also have heard it said that being altruistic, that is, doing something for someone else that doesn't benefit yourself is the highest level of good. However, is that even possible? If you define selfish as satisfying one or more of your needs, then how is it possible not to be selfish? The question is not whether you are selfish or not, it is are you selfish in a manner that hurts other people, has no effect on other people or helps other people? Think about it. Even if you had more money than you knew what to do with and you decided to give $1,000 away at the shopping mall and you slipped $1,000 into someone's purse without them knowing that you did it would that be altruistic? That would probably meet the definition of altruism; however, in doing so you satisfied the need to be altruistic. So it really was a selfish act. It was just a selfish act that benefited someone else. In this case the person who received $1,000 would probably be very happy. Even if you don't agree with my definition of selfish I think you would agree that it is not reasonable to think an individual would exhibit a behavior that doesn't satisfy one or more of their needs.

Have you ever known anyone to say, "Gee I wish I had less," or "I wish I had an older bicycle," or "I wish my car wasn't as good as it is," or "I wish that my house roof leaked"? I've never heard that. I've never met anyone who wants less. They always would like to improve their situation. Wanting more doesn't mean they're greedy it just means that they would like to be better off than they are. There's nothing wrong with that. I remember a lady saying to me years ago, "I wish I had what you have and you had something better." A very nice way of saying she would like to have more. So if you accept the fact that everyone would like more, a better bike, a better education, a better house to live in, a better car to drive, a better job, etc. and if you would like a better life you need to decide how you will do it. My suggestion to you is that you get what you want by getting others what they want in the process. This is another way of saying that creating a win-win scenario has a better chance of being successful than a win-lose scenario. If you create a win scenario for both the person you wish to serve as well as yourself how could you not be successful? Early in my life I understood this principle but didn't know how to put it into practice. I didn't know how I could get others what they wanted. I tried but was relatively unsuccessful. I finally discovered why. I was trying to give them things that I thought they needed. But what they thought they needed and what I thought they needed were different. Somehow I stumbled onto a process called "Selling through needs satisfaction." I believe it may be a sales course I attended and the following is a brief summary. The reason I'm presenting it here is that it doesn't make much sense to reinvent the wheel. As I wrote earlier, there are three ways to learn and the easiest is from the experience of others. Selling through needs satisfaction is a very good system, to the point and very effective. This process consists of three skills: Probing, Reinforcing and Closing.

PROBING

Probing involves asking questions. There are two kinds of questions to ask: open ended and closed ended. Open ended questions are just that. They give a person the chance to say whatever they want to tell you by asking them an open ended question. For example, you might say, "Tell me about yourself." That's an example of an open ended question. A closed ended question is answerable by yes or no or a choice that you give them. An example of this is, "Do you prefer chocolate or strawberry ice cream?" Asking a person a question is the best way of finding out what they want. This may sound simple but I was on a sales call with a former vice president of marketing of a large publicly traded company. This person said to me, "I wish there was a way we could find out what they want." At first I thought he was kidding. I said, "Well, we could ask them." His response was, "We can do that?" Not only can we do it we must do it. How else will we know what they want? Probing is an important skill to develop in every phase of your life.

When applying for entrance to a school, during the interview it might be good to ask the interviewer, "What kind of student are you looking for?" Be attentive to what they say such as, "I wish I could select students I knew would be successful," or "I would like to choose students who have a burning desire to learn." If the interviewer says,

"I really would like to choose the best applicant because we only have so many positions available," you could respond by saying, "I can understand how that can be a problem. Do I understand you properly, you don't want to waste a seat in your freshmen class for someone who isn't going to be successful?" Wait for verification of what you think you understand them to have said. Then tell them why you will be successful.

Once selected it would be helpful to ask your instructors what is needed to earn an A. You might discover that it's easier for you to get a better grade on a term paper if you know what the instructor wants.

If you are looking for a job it might be beneficial to know what your potential employer expects from his employees. You might ask this potential employer, "What qualities make for an exceptional employee?" These probing questions help you to uncover the person's wants and needs so that you may discover opportunities for you to help them.

REINFORCING

The second skill is reinforcing what they say are their wants or needs. Restate what you think you heard to verify its accuracy. For example, the teacher who says to you, "It's very difficult for me when I get 300 term papers in the last two weeks." You might say, "I can understand how that might be a problem. It has to be very difficult to find the time to grade all those papers. Would it be helpful to you to have those papers handed in earlier in the semester?"

If someone interviewing you for a job said, "I want someone who is a low maintenance employee, an employee that I know is going to show up on time and do the job that is required," this is the time to restate what you think you've heard, verifying its accuracy and explaining how you could satisfy their needs.

CLOSING

The third skill is closing or having the person to agree to accept your win-win solution to satisfying their wants or needs. In sales terminology this is called "closing." For example, you might say to the teacher, "Would it be OK if I handed in my term paper at the end of this month? I know it's early but maybe that would help you." In the case of applying to a college, you might say to the interviewer, "It is very important for me to be successful because I understand the choices that I make in my education will determine the quality of my life when I graduate. If you accept me I will do my best to make sure I am here the second semester by studying to the best of my ability and my past record shows that I can do that."

To an employer, you might say, "Punctuality is important to me. I am a fast learner and I take my responsibilities seriously." You might also add that your granddad told you that no matter what you do, do it to the best of your ability. Either way, your integrity and your pride are at stake.

Probing, Reinforcing and Closing sound simple but require skill and practice. There's one other area that's very important to being successful with this technique, and that is recognizing the attitudes of those to whom you are speaking. There are four basic attitudes to recognize. It is important to differentiate one from the other because they each require a different method to resolve the concern. For example, if the attitude is indifference and you provide proofs, you will fail.

ACCEPTANCE

Acceptance is the first attitude. This is the easiest. This simply means someone says, "Well that sounds good to me. Yes I'd love for you to hand in your term paper early," or "I will give you a chance to prove what you say by admitting you to our school," or "You have the job;

please show me that I made the right selection." With an attitude of acceptance all that is required is to say thank you and then be quiet.

SKEPTICISM

Skepticism is the second attitude. Skepticism means the person doesn't believe what you're telling them. They don't believe that you will hand in your term paper at the end of the month. They don't believe you will be there the second semester. They doubt you will be an exemplary employee. As my mom said, "the proof is in the pudding." If an attitude of skepticism is preventing them from making the right decision, they require proof. A proof can be a hard proof such as facts and figures that will attest to what you have said is true. In some cases, this may be a letter of reference or recommendation, a transcript or a bold statement such as, "If you hire me and you aren't satisfied with my work the first week you don't have to pay me." I know that law probably requires them to pay you, but saying that shows you are willing to walk your talk.

INDIFFERENCE

Indifference is the third attitude. There are two reasons why people are indifferent. The first reason is they may be getting this product or service or whatever it is you're talking about from someone else. In this case, you would have to demonstrate that you can do it better than their current provider. Be aware that this service or product might be provided by their spouse, relative or friend. The second reason they are indifferent is because they don't see a need for whatever it is you're talking about. If that is in relationship to a job you want you must explain to them why they should hire you. It might increase their income, make their job easier, make them more effective, more efficient, give them more time off, etc. You are giving them reasons why hiring you would benefit them.

DRAWBACK

Drawback is the last attitude. Drawbacks are perceived undesirable effects of what you are presenting. Drawbacks occur because of two reasons. The first reason is because of a misunderstanding. To address this attitude you need to probe and determine if they understand what it is that you were talking about and if not, resolve the misunderstanding. The other reason for a drawback is because it takes too much time or costs too much money. You often hear people say they won't purchase something because it is too expensive. The fact is no one really cares what something costs, what they care about is its value. Value is equal to quality divided by cost. (Perceived) Value = Quality (perceived)/Cost.

If the perceived value is high enough the purchase price is relatively less important. For example, a drawback to hiring you might be that you live far away from your place of employment. To counter act this you would first minimize the drawback. You might say, "I know I live far away but I use that time to listen to educational recordings so that I can improve my performance at work." So again, you minimize the drawback and maximize the benefit of hiring you.

Getting what you want by getting others what they want through "Needs Satisfaction" is something that can also be used in your personal relationships. Any relationship will only endure if it is symbiotic in nature. It may only be symbiotic if each party knows and fulfills the needs of the other.

Please understand that this process of uncovering needs and wants, reinforcing these perceived needs and wants and closing should not be manipulative. It is much easier to get what you want as a byproduct of serving others. The better you are at serving others, the better your needs will be met. It is actually the behavior exhibited by living by the "Golden Rule" which is, "Do unto others as you would have them do unto you."

I'm sure you have used these principles a time or two. Write one way this might help you in the near future.

_____

_____

_____

_____

_____

_____

_____

TERRY HERRON, Registered Investment Advisor and Owner of a Wealth Management Practice:

When you are working for yourself you get to choose the opportunities that you encounter. People are generally either givers or takers. I am a giver. I strive to give more than I receive. The best reward is knowing that you did the right thing. Sometimes I spend too much time on a project just because it is the right thing to do. I got this attitude from my parents. It was ingrained in me from early childhood. My dad was a Little League baseball coach. There is nothing more rewarding than helping a bunch of kids. My mother was always involved in church or school activities. So, I think I followed by example of giving of themselves.

Additionally, most folks want to have harmony in all components of their life. Part of this is working with people whose thoughts, desires and wishes are congruent with your own. I believe life is too short not to be able to enjoy my clients' company.

I am fortunate to be able to choose my clients. This is one of the ways I facilitate harmony in my life. My first priority is to understand their needs, wants and desires. The better I understand these things, the better I can design a program to meet those needs in a cost effective manner. And the better I do this, the more business it generates. Gaining confidence in my ability to give my clients what they want has helped me to serve them better. It is very satisfying to help others in a way that is mutually beneficial in all the aspects of our lives.

COMMENTS: *(Note 1)* An example of the value = quality / cost happened to me several years ago. I wanted to obtain a good telescope. I thought I might spend as much as $500. I went to the telescope store and told the sales person I wanted to test each telescope comparing one to another. I didn't want to know the price so as not to be influenced by it. I finally determined the telescope I wanted. The sales person said it cost $1200! I thought I was hearing incorrectly. I gave her every reason why I shouldn't pay that much. She turned and pointed to a sign that read, "When you buy the best, you only cry once." How true. I have enjoyed using the telescope ever since.

(Note 2): If you want to read a success story of how you can get what you want by getting others what they want, read about Richard Branson's story. He was not well off as a child, dropped out of school and developed businesses that resulted in his becoming a billionaire! His companies now number over 200. All this occurred as a result of getting others what they wanted, and doing that very well.

∼Chapter 19∼

EFFICIENCY AND EFFECTIVENESS

Efficiency refers to getting done whatever it is you have to do in a manner that uses the least amount of resources and takes the least amount of time which is one of those resources. Those who strive to be efficient do so because it takes less energy and things get done more quickly leaving time for other things.

Effectiveness refers to how well you do what you do. Effectiveness has to do with how well you accomplish the intended objectives. This may sound simple but many companies today become efficient to the detriment of effectiveness. The most obvious example is calling a business. The automated answer will tell you, "Your call is very important to us. Please stay on the line. Your call will be answered in the order in which it was received." They may be saying that your call is important to them but while on hold you start to believe that maybe your call is not important. This may be very efficient for them but, it is not very effective for the consumer. The business may think they're doing a good job but the consumer is likely to attempt to meet their requirements someplace else. No matter what endeavor you are involved in, it is good to ask yourself, "Am I being as efficient as possible and still being effective?"

The above begs the question, "Who measures efficiency and effectiveness?" I suppose it could be various people or groups. Each of us has a responsibility to ourselves and those we serve to be as efficient and effective as we can. Those we serve include ourselves, our employer, our customers and society in general. Being as efficient and effective as is feasible benefits everyone. Doing so gives you a good feeling. Being efficient and effective gets things done while they are important avoiding the anxiety of waiting until they become urgent as well. This will help you to reduce the anxiety often associated with meeting deadlines. You are keeping those things that are both important and urgent to a minimum.

Not taking sufficient time to do homework may be efficient but may not be effective. You got done quickly but what was the quality of your work? What are other examples?

_____

_____

_____

_____

_____

AMY KING, Physician Assistant:

As physician assistant, I am well aware of the importance of being both efficient and effective. I work in a very busy practice where both are critical. I see patients, answer phone calls, review labs and important patient documents sometimes within a matter of minutes. My patients have busy lives and if I make them wait in my office for extended periods, I am not being respectful of their time. This requires me to be efficient with my time management. However, I must also be accurate (effective) in my diagnosis and treatment or you probably wouldn't care if I was efficient. If you see me for strep throat and I don't give you the right antibiotic or instructions regarding how to take the medication, I am no longer effective and you continue to be sick.

My efficiency and effectiveness also affects the people I work with. If I am slow seeing patients, answering phone calls etc. due to my lack of organization, the other providers have to pick up the slack for my inefficiencies. If I am trying to be efficient and quickly get through my paperwork, patient laboratory results etc. as quickly as possible, I might make the wrong diagnosis or give the patient the wrong information, therefore, potentially seriously hurting my patient. I may have been efficient as my work was "done" but not effective in helping my patient with their health issue.

What I do at my job can be a life or death situation. Efficiency is a must as I need to get through my daily tasks in a reasonable time and have time for my family. However, if I am not effective I could seriously hurt someone which is another undesirable outcome which is why efficiency and effectiveness go hand in glove for me.

COMMENTS: When you are efficient at doing something it leaves more time for other things. It is really one of the ways to manage your time. But it is also important to be effective, that is doing whatever you are doing well. So, efficiency and effectiveness seem to go together. One without the other is not as good as both together. Putting this another way, if you are playing basketball it might be good for your team to get a shot off quickly in order to get more shots throughout the game. The more shots your team takes the better your chances of scoring more points than your opponent. That would be efficient. But it would be good if the majority of the shots taken went in the basket. That's effectiveness. They work better together.

～Chapter 20～

DIFFERENTIAL ADVANTAGE

Differential advantage is a business term which means establishing the reason someone would use one particular product or service over another. Durability, appearance, cost, uniqueness, availability, service, etc., are examples of what might be an advantage a business believes is characteristic of their product or service that differentiates them from their competitors. It gives a business an advantage over their competitors in selling their service or product. That is why it is called a "differential advantage."

The manufacturer of the Volvo automobile believes that safety is its main competitive advantage so that's what they emphasize in their ads. Mercedes Benz believes that "German engineering" is its differential advantage so that's what they emphasize in their ads. Maytag, the manufacturer of kitchen appliances, believes its differential advantage is reliability. So their ads show a Maytag repair man with nothing to do. Having a differential advantage is critical to the success of a company. It gives it a competitive edge. But a differential advantage is not just important for businesses it's important for individuals as well.

Why would a school admit you over someone else? Why would an employer hire you over other applicants? Isn't it good enough just to say you're just as good as anyone else? Would you have a better chance if you are better than the other candidates? These are examples of where having a differential advantage becomes important. Your differential advantage might be your personality, your education, your work experience or your work ethic. Maybe your differential advantage is your understanding that you are interdependent with others. This combined with your ability to lead and create effective and efficient teams will give you the edge you need. In an interview, for example, you might ask your future employer what they think the perfect employee would be like. Or, what it is they would like you to accomplish rather than asking them what they can do for you. Asking these questions sincerely might be a differential advantage for you since you might be the only candidate to ask them. You would be demonstrating an interest in learning how you might be able to benefit your employer rather than how your employer might benefit to you. Understanding principles of human behavior, nature and commerce might be a huge differential advantage for you since so few people seem to grasp them. All things being equal, your differential advantages are what separate you from your competitors and will help you to succeed.

List important "Differential Advantages" you have created or want to create in your life.

_____

_____

_____

_____

_____

_____

_____

MEGAN ERICKSON, Student, age 20:

Right out of high school, I began working my first job. The timing and location were perfect, which made me question my luck. My application was good, but it wasn't stellar. Looking back, it was clear why I got the position. The store manager asked when I was available, and I told her all summer, any day, any shift.

That was a start. It was rough going for a while, even though I was only working three days a week. When others called in sick, or didn't show up, I worked their shifts. There was a list of duties near the register, and I went through the tasks daily, without prompting and regardless of who the manager on duty was.

The end of the summer was near, and I was going to be moving into a dorm room, an hour away. I was asked if I could continue working at the store, for breaks and for a few weekends.

I agreed, having been unsure of whether I would have to stop working there once school started.

I have worked there for almost two years now. Co-workers come and go, rules change, school continues. While I started off with only a few days a week, it became normal for me to work five days a week (despite my part time status). My bosses have been amazing and supportive of my schedule.

I am incredibly thankful to have such a steady job. Most of my peers have already gone through several jobs, and have to search again every summer. My differential advantage was my work ethic and availability. Working at this store isn't easy, nor does it pay a lot; however, from the start, I was determined to prove myself, and to gain great references. Many employees quit early on, call off regularly, or lounge around instead of working. I never saw the point in doing so—if you're going to do something, you might as well give it your all. I like knowing that I will continue to have this job, get more hours than most, and have support for when I am ready to move on to the next step of my life.

DAN TORSELL, Ski Resort President and General Manager:

I learned about differential advantage shortly after graduating from college when I went to work for Killington ski area. The founder and owner, Preston Smith, fully comprehended the concept of differential advantage. He designed the snow making equipment and was proud of the pursuit of perfecting snow-making and the large number of trails. So, Killington became the resort with trails for every level of skier and the best snow. I most recently worked at another ski area in the East. Our differential was great facilities and an increased quality in the skiing experience on and off the mountain.

So, a differential advantage is offering something that will create an interest and desire to participate in an activity. In our case it is skiing on our mountain. Increased usage will help us to slowly grow so we can continue to provide a high quality skiing and boarding experience. This is not easy as we are surrounded by world class ski areas. But our differential is that skiing here is about skiing as it was meant to be, peaceful, beautiful and not crowded. We are a family oriented ski area. You can bring your grandkids here and know they will have a great time and not get run over by other skiers and boarders. I recently had two friends from the east come out for a visit. They brought a gentleman with them who grew up near Torino Ski Resort in Italy. He skied here and was flabbergasted. "It is so peaceful here," he said, "I'm bringing my grandkids here!" This is a short example of how a differential is important to me and the execution of my duties for the ski area.

COMMENTS: Differential advantage is not just for businesses. You will need to have a differential advantage in just about anything you do. Why would you make the team, get into a school, date a particular person, get a job, etc. Why not someone else? It will be because of why you should be chosen over someone else, your differential advantage. So, create and promote those advantages.

∽ Chapter 21 ∽

FACTORS THAT DETERMINE YOUR INCOME

The educational phase of your life is work, hard work. Get used to it because it's true of every phase of life. Work is a word that is generally used to describe the expenditure of energy, physical or mental, in the attempt to complete a particular task. Whether work is fun or enjoyable or satisfying is up to you. There is work that you will do because you're part of a family and that is what's required. For some of those tasks you may or may not be paid. At some point you may seek a job for which you will be paid. It may be mowing lawns, babysitting, working in a store or some other job. Later, after you have completed the educational phase of your life you will seek employment that is "permanent." Employment that hopefully, you may consider to be a career and not just a job.

A very important question to ask, whether you have a job or a career, is what determines your income. Occasionally, in the news, you will hear that people are going on strike to obtain a higher salary. You'll hear discussion regarding increasing the minimum wage. But what are the factors that really determine your level of income? As far as I can tell there are just three. I suppose you could add a fourth one which would be luck or special circumstances such as working for your grandpa, but obviously that will not typically be the case. So, let's talk about the three factors that determine your level of income.

The first factor is **how difficult it is to replace you.** One of the reasons why McDonald's workers periodically attempt to strike or demonstrate for increased wages is because they feel they're not being paid what they're worth. However, is that the case? Does the employer really determine what they pay or is it the market place that determines the rate of pay? Jobs at fast food restaurants are usually known as entry level jobs. These jobs pay what the market determines is required to pay to obtain employees. In other words, if they're making "X" dollars and they continue to be employed then both the employer and employee are saying this is the necessary salary to have someone continue to do this job.

Every employer wants to make as great a profit as possible. Even "non-profits" usually strive to have their income be equal to or greater than their expenses. Generally speaking they are not concerned about paying their employees the greatest salary possible. They pay what they have to pay to attract employees. If an employee leaves can they replace that employee? Can they find sufficient employees willing to work at the rate of pay they are offering? So the first principle that determines your level of income is how difficult it is to replace you. In the cases mentioned above, it is relatively easy to replace these employees since there is an abundance of people willing to take the job. This drives down the salary that businesses have to pay their employees.

The second principal that determines your income is **your value to society**. This is not an objective view but a subjective judgment of society. Society's values are not always what you would think they should be. That is why popular entertainers makes more money than a teacher. Our society values them more than they value a teacher or firemen or a paramedic or a police officer. Personally, I would rather have a good police force than to hear a popular entertainer perform in my home town, but that's just me. So it isn't the objective value to a society that determines your income but how much people in that society are willing to pay for a particular product or service.

The third principle that determines your income is **how well you do what you do**. A friend of mine is a welder and does very well financially because he is a very good welder. This isn't a complicated principle; he does what he does better than just about anyone else. If you're mowing lawns and do a better job than anyone else you will be able to charge more than others. Clean off the driveway, edge it, do the trimming, do it promptly and you'll probably do those things better than anyone else and therefore you can charge more. I hope that you will find an occupation where it is very difficult to replace you, you are valued by society and you do what you do better than anyone else.

These three principles are why neurosurgeons have a greater income than entry level employees. You can use these principles to your advantage during any of the phases of your life. Do things that people don't expect you to do. Exceed their expectations making it more difficult to replace you. Do what they value and do it better than anyone else.

List ways you may increase your "Value."

COMMENTS: When I owned my business I had about 200 employees. Some employees were aides (folks with at least a high school education) and would help with tasks that didn't take a college education. Some were receptionists who had to have good verbal communication skills. Others were responsible for billing for services rendered. And some were physical therapists (college educated and licensed in the state where they worked).

It was a small company and did not have a pay scale policy and procedure. I paid what the market place demanded. The aides required the least education and applicants for that position were plentiful. Their training was on the job training, they usually didn't have any prior skills or experience. They were paid the least because of this. Receptionists were paid a bit better as they were required to have some experience and there were fewer applicants. Billing for services required prior experience and skills. Therefore, these folks were paid according to their skills.

Physical therapists were more difficult to find. They had skills that took longer to acquire and for some, to be considered for a director's position additional skills were required. These factors and the urgency of my need for this category of employee drove the salary upward.

Additionally, what I considered "low maintenance employees" were paid more. After all, they made my life easier. I wanted to retain their services. They did what they did better and more reliably than others. They were worth more to me. This is how the factors mentioned above work in real life.

~Chapter 22~

VISION STORY

A number of personal improvement and business experts have said that a goal is much more likely to be achieved if it is written. An unwritten goal is a whim, a dream. Joel Barker, a futurist, stated, "Vision without action is dreaming. Action without vision is random activity. Vision and action together can change the world." A vision story is an attempt to bring reality to your dreams, hopes, and desires. These need to be achievable and moderated by what is possible. A vision story is a living document (which means it changes as you change; it grows with you) produced through visioning which brings clarity of purpose to your life's direction. It is as though you are writing a screen play of your life the way you would like it to be in the future. That might be next year, five years from now or ten years from now. It might be easiest to begin this process with looking at your life the way you would like it to be next year.

The vision story creates a picture story. It comes from the heart. It is as Bobby Kennedy, former Attorney General of the United States, stated, "Some see things the way they are and ask, *Why?* I see things as I'd like them to be and ask, *Why not?*" Most of us will, at one time or another, think about the future. Wouldn't it be fun to be able to predict what will happen? The process of visioning and developing a vision story attempts to do just that, predicting the future by creating it. As Kevin B. Carmony said, "Most men add a new page to their book of life with each passing day. The wise man simply lives out what he has already written." This statement makes great sense. A vision story is helpful no matter what your age. It is like a dream, only you are awake. When you are dreaming, your dream seems like reality until you awake. Visioning is making your dreams come true by making them goals and incorporating them into your vision story. They are written and cause you to take action so your dreams become reality. The visioning process will work so well you may have to pinch yourself to make sure you are not dreaming.

If you are in grade school you could begin with looking at what you would like to accomplish the next year. Maybe it would be to learn how to play a particular piece on the piano, improve your math skills, achieve a higher level of skill in some physical activity such as skiing or snowboarding.

Try to imagine what that would be like on a date of your choosing. It is your vision. Make the image as real as possible. Where will you play the piano? Who will be in the audience (if you want one)? What will you wear? How will it feel to walk to the piano, to feel the keys? What will you hear? How will it smell? Imagine playing this piece, hitting every note perfectly, making the piano sing. You feel very good about your playing. How does that feel? Do the same with every aspect of your vision story. See yourself as you would like to be. Make it real to make it happen.

Maybe you want to improve your math skills. How will you demonstrate your improvement with math skills? Will it be on a test, in the class room or some other place? The visioning process for this is the same as for playing the piano. Make it real; vision everything as you would like it to be.

In high school you might have slightly different goals. In 9th grade your immediate goal might be to make it to 10th grade next year. You are older and the choices you make have a larger impact on the quality of your life. Therefore, you might also have longer term goals. You might want to be accepted to a particular college or trade school. You might want to win a varsity letter or develop a high degree of expertise in something. The process of creating your vision story is the same. Imagine what you want your life to be like as you graduate from high school with distinction. Imagine you have earned varsity letters. Imagine you have been accepted to the school of your choice.

Later in life this process will be just as valuable to your success. You will imagine your life as you would like it to be 5, 10 or even 20 years in the future. You will be creating the future you want for yourself. The more real you make your vision story by using all your senses and the more detailed your vision story, the more likely you are to achieve the life you want. One of the keys to a happy life is having dreams. One of the keys to a successful life is making dreams come true. Visioning is an important part of creating a successful life. It facilitates making dreams become reality.

Begin writing your living Vision Story here. It is just a beginning. Your vision will grow and change over time. You might use a note book to chronicle your vision story.

How would you describe your life one, five, or ten years from now?

_____

_____

_____

_____

_____

_____

MARK ADAMSON, owner of haircutting franchises:

I have not just been keeping my thoughts positive but enthusiastically using my thoughts to achieve my goals and desires. I know that whatever I think of expands. Realizing this, I have become vigilant about thinking positive thoughts about how I would like my life to be.

This is easier said than done but I am getting better at governing what I think about. It is so much easier to default to negative thinking. It has taken years of work to think about what I want my life to be like. I focus on this through visualization, seeing my life as I would like it to be.

Every day I meditate while I exercise focusing upon my goals. I think about how it would feel to achieve my business, *financial, spiritual and relationship goals. I have found that the better I visualize these goals the more likely I am to achieve them in the real world.*

COMMENTS: Creating a vision story can be very helpful in helping you to live the life you wish to live. It begins with seeing in your mind's eye what your life will be like at some time in the future. Napoleon Hill said, "What the mind of man can conceive and believe, it can achieve." Writing your vision story will cause you to do the things necessary to achieve your vision. It is a living document and can and should change as circumstances and desires change. The point is that a vision story, your vision story, facilitates your living the kind of life you want to lead. It is well worth the effort and it can be fun as well.

Years ago I was sitting in my spa looking at the mountains and the person I was with asked me if I ever imagined I would be living in this house, sitting outside looking at the mountains. My answer was, "Yes, it is just as I imagined it." I believe my vision of living in a mountain home was what made it happen. Visioning works.

∼Chapter 23∼

GOALS

Zig Ziegler, a business consultant, once said, "You gotta have goals." Steve Covey says, "Begin with the end in mind." However you say it, having goals is very necessary if you want to lead a successful life. A goal is something you want to achieve. It requires plans and commitment to the end point that you desire. You should have short and long term goals. They don't need to be monumental goals. They can be something as simple as getting homework done the day it is assigned. A goal for something that requires more time and thought might be to have completed that goal in two weeks. Your goals might be to go skiing or biking on a particular day or to complete your music lesson. Having goals makes it more likely that you will live a successful life.

A prestigious eastern university did a study whose intention, I believe, was to show that going to that particular school had great value because people did very well after graduating. What they discovered was something worth noting. Those who did not have goals made an average of X dollars per year. Those who had goals but had not written them down made an average of 3X dollars per year. Those who had goals and had written them down had a salary of 10X dollars. That alone would make me want to write down my goals. I hope you take that point as well.

Writing your goals is important whether they are short term or long term, small or large goals. As you proceed through your educational experience you may want to further your education. Your long term goal when you're in 9th grade could be to achieve the grades necessary for college admission. Later, one of your long term goals may be to own a home in a certain area, or to achieve a certain income. A personal goal might be to learn to play the guitar or to climb a particular mountain or ski so many days. A spiritual goal might be to read some specific books related to spirituality. A financial goal might be to obtain a certain amount of wealth by a specific age.

I suggest you begin with some short term goals. Such as completing your homework on the day it is assigned. Perhaps a short term goal could be cleaning your room on a certain day. It could also be studying music lessons or reading for a certain number of hours. You determine what goals you think are appropriate for you on a short term basis. Short term might be weekly. Later in your life a short term goal might take a year to achieve. Begin with what you believe to be appropriate short term goals and write them down on a calendar. A day timer is better but we'll discuss that later. Establish short term goals for each component of your being: Personal, Professional, Spiritual and Financial. During the educational phase of your life learning is your responsibility. That is what you are supposed to do. So write your goals for this phase of your life.

Develop long term goals for yourself which might extend several months into the future. These goals might be to achieve a certain grade point average the current semester. A long term goal might be to learn a certain number of songs to play on an instrument the next six months. Maybe a long term goal would be to learn some new activity or to gain some expertise in a particular area the next six months. Another might be to save a certain amount of money over the next year. You pick the long term goals that are important to you and write them down.

The more specific you are about what it is that you want and the more detail in which you write these goals, the more likely you are to achieve them. As you get better at determining what goals you wish to achieve your goals can expand in nature. Dream big, shoot high. Poet Robert Browning said, "A man's reach should exceed his grasp or what's a heaven for?" What you do in the educational phase of your life will determine the level of income and the level of success you will achieve throughout your life.

Begin by establishing a time frame for your short term and long term goals. Short term goals could be goals that are weekly, quarterly and then annually. Your long term goals can begin with a monthly time frame, which then stretch to quarterly, annually and maybe two and three year goals and eventually five to ten year goals.

Below list a few of your short term goals.

_____

_____

_____

_____

_____

_____

_____

Below are a few of your long term goals.

_____

_____

_____

_____

_____

_____

_____

RODNEY FENSKE, Sheriff:

One of the reasons I ran for the office of sheriff was that I didn't like the way the department was run. If I didn't have goals nothing would happen. And I couldn't wait for things to happen, I had to make them happen. I found it necessary to change personnel, set standards and hire people. I wanted people who had good judgment and could make good decisions, were local people, friendly and could talk to people.

I hired a competent undersheriff and together we trained new personnel and taking individual differences into account, held them accountable for their behavior. I am very accessible to my staff and the public as well.

One of my long term goals is to complete the building of a new justice center. Our current jail was built in 1955 and doesn't meet our current needs or comply with new laws and regulations. Another goal is to continue training and updating our infrastructure so we may be both efficient and effective. Laws and regulations change frequently and training is the only way to keep up with them. The only way to keep the department running the way I like is to establish reasonable goals and bring them to fruition.

COMMENTS: I was editor of our company newsletter. I wrote an article stating how a goal that was not written was a wish and not a goal. For a goal to be achieved it needed to be written. I was challenged by a regional vice-president of our company. In our company newsletter he wrote: "Show me how a busy person has the time to set goals and how this can work and I will eat my hat."

I took the challenge. For many years I wanted to visit Alaska. I thought about it but it never seemed to happen. I was too busy. Every day came and went but I was so involved with my daily activities that I put off planning a trip to Alaska.

The first thing I did was to announce in the next company newsletter that my goal was to visit Alaska. The next obvious step was to decide when I would do this. That meant setting a date which I did and recorded in my day timer (calendar). After consulting with my family, it would be August 12 and everyone would go. How would we get there? It would be by air of course. But when would I need to make reservations? At least six months ahead. That would be February 12. So, I wrote that in my day timer as well. How much would it cost? After determining what it would cost a portion of every paycheck was put aside. All of these things were recorded in my day timer at the appropriate time before the "go to Alaska" date. You can see how it worked. I established a goal and reduced it to writing along with all the things that had to be done to make this happen. Putting it in writing made the process more obvious and dating what needed to be done made it easier. I didn't have to think about every detail. I just had to refer to my day timer. My entire family went to Alaska within the year! After years of wishing I would go to Alaska, the challenge and writing my goal caused it to happen. I don't think the regional vice-president ate his hat, perhaps he did eat a little crow.

~Chapter 24~

SWOT

Imagine that you were blindfolded, your hearing suppressed and you were taken on an airplane ride. When you landed, if you were asked, "Where you would like to go?" The first question you would probably ask is, "Where am I?" The same is true in deciding to lead an intentional life. The place to start is to determine where you are before you establish where you would like to go. This is done by performing a SWOT analysis. SWOT is short for, Strengths, Weaknesses, Opportunities and Threats. Generally, Strengths and Weaknesses are considered to be internal factors that you possess. Opportunities and Threats are generally considered to be external to you. They are factors over which you have little or no control.

A SWOT analysis is a tool which will help you to achieve whatever it is you want to achieve in life. It's something you should do multiple times in your life as circumstances continually change and therefore your SWOT analysis will change as well. Performing a

SWOT will help you to objectively identify those factors that will assist you in achieving your goals. These are building blocks for your success plan.

STRENGTHS

Begin with a review of your strengths. List anything you believe is a strength you possess. Strengths are those factors that would cause a friend, a teacher, an employer, someone who is important in your life to list as those things that make them want to be associated with you. They could include things like intelligence, attitude, honesty, high energy, enthusiasm, your educational experiences, or athletic ability. They might also include your physical appearance, sense of humor, your calmness, or your strong work ethic. You may be empathetic, a good listener, a quick learner, a good communicator. You may have leadership abilities. You may be persistent and possess other factors. Depending on your age you can ask for help in identifying your strengths. You could ask your mom, or dad, teacher, an employer — whomever you respect and you feel knows you well enough to give you some objective input. Be prepared for some input you might not like to hear. Your strengths are important to identify. Once they have been identified, it doesn't mean that you want to rest on your laurels and not change anything. It means you want to take those strengths and make them an even stronger part of your life. A part of your life that helps you to move in the direction you desire.

What are some of your Strengths?

_____

_____

_____

_____

_____

_____

_____

WEAKNESSES

Weaknesses are just what the term implies. Weaknesses are likely to limit or inhibit your ability to succeed. By identifying your weakness you will be able to formulate and implement a plan to reduce, eliminate or turn your weaknesses into strengths. For example, if a lack of experience is a problem in future employment, you could turn that weakness into a strength by realizing that a lack of experience enables you to be more open minded and therefore, you don't have preconceived ideas regarding how something should be done. But weaknesses are not easy to deal with because it is not comfortable to face what might be considered a deficit in your being. I was once speaking with the director of an outpatient rehabilitation facility who was listing his strengths. An employee knocked on the door, opened it and asked, "May I speak to you for a moment?" The director replied, "How many times have I told you that when that door is closed, I don't want to be disturbed. I will talk to you later." The director of the clinic then turned to me and said, "Oh yes, one of my strengths is communication skills."

It is important to be as objective as you can. One of your weaknesses might be that you procrastinate or put things off. For some their motto could be, "Why do today what you can put off until tomorrow?" A weakness might be that you cave into social pressure. In order to keep a friend or be a part of a group you do something you know isn't right or you don't want to do. It might be that you do not receive constructive criticism very well. If that is true, the next suggestion might be difficult to attempt. You might ask your parents, a friend, or an employer to help you identify your weaknesses. But be careful because this can be very threatening. It is never easy to hear about your own weaknesses. But the purpose of this exercise is to identify those weaknesses and develop a plan to minimize your weaknesses or turn them into strengths. If you're a procrastinator, make a sincere effort to get off the starting line and do whatever needs to be done as soon as it is assigned or as soon as you can do it. Successful individuals are individuals who can get a lot done. This is generally because these folks don't put things off. They do what needs to be done immediately. Then they can forget about that particular task and move on to another task.

What are some of your Weaknesses?

_____

_____

_____

_____

_____

_____

_____

I think you can see why strengths and weaknesses are generally considered to be something that occurs within yourself. Those are things over which you have control and can change if you so desire.

Opportunities and Threats are generally thought to be external to you. They are those factors over which you have little or no control. But as you read through the following, I hope you realize this is not always the case. Many things that are considered to be out of your control actually are within your control.

OPPORTUNITIES

What opportunities exist for you? Sometimes people say they feel sorry for younger people because there are so few opportunities for them. I don't think these people are being objective in their appraisal of what opportunities actually exist. Opportunities that exist today are more numerous than existed only several years ago. They just require a bit more creativity and flexibility. For example, I met a woman who had a college degree in wildlife biology. There's not a great job market for wildlife biology. Most people with that degree find some other type of work. She wanted to work in the field of wildlife biology. She discovered that in every land exchange where the government is trading some governmental property for privately held property the government requires an impact study be done. Part of that impact study is how the proposed land exchange would affect wildlife. So, she was able to talk herself into a position with a group of attorneys who dealt with land exchange between the government and an independent agency. The government requires the impact study. She loves wildlife and enjoys doing wildlife impact studies. The attorneys enjoy writing and negotiating contracts but dislike doing wildlife impact studies. She created a perfect match.

This is an example of looking for opportunities and making that opportunity happen. List opportunities that exist or you create for yourself. You can include educational opportunities, opportunities to go to a particular camp, to learn a particular skill, to meet with people who would like to act as your mentor. An opportunity might be to shadow someone at work to find out what type of work you may like to do. After all, the purpose of an education is to develop for yourself a responsible and productive life. As you start listing these opportunities the list will become almost endless and as Ralph Waldo Emerson stated, "Do not follow where the path may lead, go instead where there is no path and leave a trail." Keep that in mind when you list your opportunities.

What Opportunities do you see for yourself?

_____

_____

_____

_____

_____

_____

_____

THREATS

The *T* in SWOT stands for threats. Threats are those things that might inhibit you from achieving whatever it is you wish to achieve. Threats might include a lack of education, a lack of skill, difficulty in having enough money to start a business, strong competition for whatever it is you want to do, whether it is entering college, taking a course, or being selected as an employee. These will exist at any point in your life's path.

List some threats you see for yourself. Turn these into opportunities wherever and whenever you can.

_____

_____

_____

_____

_____

_____

_____

For young people today, one of the threats that exist is cyberbullying. Someone might break up with a boyfriend or girlfriend and make a note to someone else. If that note is then sent into cyberspace all in the network may read it. Someone may decide to say some things about you that aren't true. But it's your choice regarding how you might respond. First of all you probably won't even know this is happening if you don't engage in social media. It is after all a choice you make. I realize you may belong and participate in one or more online social networks. But how much time you spend and how you respond to what is contained in those sites is also up to you. It's your choice.

Be an optimist. Look at threats that exist for you and decide how you will respond to them. As Franklin D. Roosevelt said, "The only limit of our realization of tomorrow will be our doubts of today." You only get one life, live your dreams.

KEN HANSEN, owner, electrical contracting business:

A SWOT analysis is helpful for me in assessing and reassessing my business. When I am asked to bid on a job I need to know my strengths as they pertain to what I am asked to do. How can I do what I'm being asked to do better than my competitors are able to do? Why would the customer choose my service over my competitors? I need to know that I can handle the job so my customer is happy and I can make a profit.

A weakness might be that we specialize in a few areas. I can't be everywhere so I need to make sure that the job is within the expertise of my crew. I can only accept work that I know I can do well and I am only as good as my crew.

I try to take advantage of the opportunities that I see. If I'm asked to bid on a job, I look for the best way to do the job and for other services I might be able to provide for the customer. Some time ago I got a call from a home owner telling me that people were getting shocked while using his pool. Not a good situation. It gave me an opportunity to analyze the situation and fix it. Other opportunities arise that give me the opportunity to diversify my services.

Threats to my service include regulations that increase the cost of the work I do when others may choose to fly under the radar and not comply with them. Knowing about SWOT analysis helps me to see what I do well and where I need to improve my business.

COMMENTS: When I first learned about SWOT I thought it meant more work for no reason. Didn't I already know what my strengths and weaknesses were? It was a real eye opener when I finally took time to sit down and actually take this exercise seriously. I learned a lot and what I learned helped me and my business.

It doesn't matter if you think of this section as SWOT or something else. It is doing the process of self-assessment that is important. It will let you know where you are in the process of life. Are you happy with where you are or are there goals you would like to achieve? Whether you are in school, studying a trade or in college, achieving your goals begins with a self-appraisal. Knowing where you are is helpful in knowing how you will get to where you want to be in all components of your being.

∼Chapter 25∼

PRIORITY AND TIME MANAGEMENT

Have you ever noticed that some people seem to get a lot more done than others and still have time to do even more? Why is that? While it is true that some have the natural ability to get more done the great equalizer is that we all have the same time. For everyone there is 24 hours in each day, 7 days each week and 52 weeks each year. So what is the difference? It is how time is used or managed. Peter Drucker, an American management consultant said, "Time is the scarcest resource and unless it's managed nothing else can be managed."

Getting things done begins with identifying what needs to be done and what would be nice to get done. List everything you need to do or want to do. Number them in order of priority, taking into consideration such things as what has the most immediate need, the time that is available, what is most urgent, etc. Then, as Stephen Covey stated, "Put first things first."

In the previous section you created a vision story. This is an important process. But just creating a vision story doesn't make these things happen. It takes work and that should include all of the previous principles in this book. Priority and time management are critical to this process. Unless you manage time it will manage you.

Your list of things you need to do while you are in K through 8th grade might include doing your homework, cleaning your room, playing, practicing the piano or sports and other activities. Place them in order of importance. You need to practice the piano if you want to achieve a higher level of expertise. But doing your homework takes priority. If you neglect to do your homework before you do other activities you might not have time to play the piano. Practicing the piano might be priority number two but you have to go to soccer practice when the practice is held, so it might become priority number three depending upon the circumstances. Cleaning your room might be another priority. If you do a few minutes each day you might not have to use a large block of time to do the cleaning which might feel overwhelming.

In high school your vision may be longer term but the process is the same. By making a list of "have to do's and nice to do's" you will be thinking critically about the relative importance of these things. You will schedule your time appropriately and will become more effective and efficient. You will be more relaxed because you will be working on things that are important but not critical or urgent! You will be in control of what you do and when you do it.

This is not to say you won't occasionally be in situations where you need to do something that is both important and urgent. But by using priority and time management techniques you will be in these situations less often.

Prioritize all your major activities. This is Priority Management. Then schedule these things on a calendar with the specific time you expect to allocate to each activity. You are now beginning to engage in Time Management.

Writing something you want to accomplish on a calendar isn't magic but it comes close. For example, you wrote on July 15 of the next year, "Climb Mt. Elbert."

If that's all you do it might not happen. But the act of writing it down might cause you to think about who will go with you. You might then write down on the appropriate date, "Get commitment from Jim, Mason and Ellie to climb Elbert with me." You might also list what equipment and supplies you would need, how to get to the trailhead, etc. Each one of these will require some planning and an entry on a calendar working backward so you will be prepared well in advance. These things will make it more likely that you will climb Mount Elbert. That's the beauty of priority and time management. There are many publications dealing with priority and time management. Find one or more you like and incorporate their suggestions into your daily life.

JAMES TAYLOR, Vice President, Colorado Mountain College:

To look at how Priority and Time Management is part of my life today requires a looking back in time. Years ago I learned to establish goals and identify critical steps to completion. Over the years, I learned that goal setting and accomplishment are the baselines that lead to a good life. As I matured and had many leadership opportunities, I have realized that goals must be prioritized, as some may be more important than others, and goals are often time dependent. It is with this time management process that real progress is made and how I have found align-ment between my accomplishments and my values.

I don't think I could be successful in my current position if I didn't use priority and time management on an ongoing basis. I have so many things that I need to do that I must prioritize them and schedule my time. On a good day I have all the time and energy needed to accomplish all my tasks and make prog-ress on projects, while also leading others. However, not every day is good and this isn't a perfect world and things come up over which I have no control. Learning to manage my time and energy and make progress on the things that matter most is critical to making progress.

I believe the earlier in life one learns how to implement and master time management and prioritization the more fulfilling your life will be. But it isn't always easy. I can think of many times in my life I have not been successful in managing time and prioritizing correctly. There have been times when I simply was out of balance. For more than 20 years I guided mountain climbing expeditions in other countries and loved to run both roads and trails. I loved running so much that I ended up run-ning 84 marathons and 36 ultra-marathons. While I found joy in running and climbing, the races, climbing and travel took me away from my family and other more important goals. As I aged I needed to manage time and energy better because I could not keep everything moving forward at the same time. In fact, I have learned to say no to some things I previously would have agreed to do and even turned down opportunities that my younger self would have been thrilled to accept.

Learning to manage time and prioritize my values has made me a better leader, father and husband. I find ways to evaluate my actions and attention and make sure that I remember what matters most in order to keep things in perspective and have a fulfilling life.

COMMENTS: When I was in high school, I was the "King of Procrastination" which is the polar opposite of using priority and time management. When Friday rolled around and I had homework that was due on Monday, I knew I had Saturday and Sunday to get it done. That left Friday free to do whatever I pleased. Saturday began with either getting ready for participation in a school sport or make up ball games at the local playground. Either of these took most of the daylight hours. Saturday evening is date night or movie night or better yet both. Pizza was mandatory after the movie. That didn't leave much time for homework but I always had Sunday. Sunday meant church in the morning and playing more ball games in the afternoon. Homework would wait until Sunday evening. Sunday evening brought really good TV programming. Well, Sunday didn't lend itself very well to doing homework. May as well watch The Ed Sullivan Show, Bonanza, Perry Como, The Smuther's Brothers and other culturally important programs.

Not much time for homework. Just deal with it. Dealing with it meant feeling anxious Sunday night and dreading Monday at school as I contemplated the impending embarrassment I would suffer. Now, you would think one would learn from this experience. But memory is short lived and when the next Friday occurred, it was another weekend filled with play, TV and not enough time for homework.

This might sound like fun but believe me if it was it didn't last very long. It was a very unsuccessful approach to the educational phase of my life and an unsuccessful lifestyle. It took me several more years to focus on what was really important in the educational phase of life and to use priority and time management techniques to help me develop a successful lifestyle. The most significant change I noticed was the absence of anxiety in my life and peacefully looking forward to class. My unsuccessful lifestyle cost around five years of my life but at least I learned the importance of focusing and using these techniques to make my life better.

Now I am in the Reflection phase of my life. I can look back and tell you that living a successful lifestyle and a continued effort to apply the principles presented in this book has had a dramatic positive effect on all the components of my life. Best of all, living these principles is one of the reasons your grandma, Nini, took an interest in me! It had a great influence on getting us together and our relationship is why you are here. And we continue to have a wonderful life together. Growing old is easy; dealing with it isn't. So it is comforting to have the Spiritual component aligned between us. And it is comforting to know we are financially secure. But we are not perfect and these principles and concepts are not easy to apply. We often fall off the horse but when we do, we get back up and ride. That has made all the difference. So, when you fall off, get back up and ride!

Our wish is for you to have an even better life than we have and we know you can, facilitated by implementing the principles and concepts in this book.

AFTERWORD

The information provided in this book is not new but it is valuable. You don't have to implement what's in this book or even know what is in this book to be successful but it will help. And who wouldn't want help? Speaking of help, there are many self-help books worthy of reading. Some of my favorite books include *How To Win Friends and Influence People,* by Dale Carnegie; *Think and Grow Rich,* by Napoleon Hill; *Looking Out For Number One,* by Robert Ringer; *Seven Habits* series by Stephen Covey and just about anything by Roger Dawson and Wayne Dyer. Some of these are very old but the principles are still very current. I have given seminars to large corporations using the principles presented in these books and was very well received. Understanding the principles and applying them will improve your chances and level of success dramatically. Like anything else it takes practice to be good at these things. I am reminded of retired professional golfer Lee Trevino. He hit the ball into a sand trap. He approached the ball and hit it out of the sand trap and into the hole. He heard a woman in the crowd say, "How lucky!" He went over to her and said, "You are right. I was lucky. But the more I practice, the luckier I get." Practice being the person you would like to be, never give up and "Get Lucky!!!"

*9 7 8 0 9 9 8 2 8 0 8 0 6 *